DICK A. STOKEN

CYCLES

What They Are, What They Mean, How to Profit by Them

McGRAW-HILL BOOK COMPANY

New York St. Louis San Francisco Auckland Bogotá Düsseldorf
Johannesburg London Madrid Mexico Montreal New Delhi Panama
Paris São Paulo Singapore Sydney Tokyo Toronto

A prophet is one who, when everyone else despairs, hopes. And when everyone else hopes he despairs. You'll ask why. It's because he has mastered the great secret: The Wheel Turns.

SLY THOMAS IN NIKOS KAZANTZAKIS'S *The Last Temptation of* Christ (Simon & Schuster, New York, 1960).

Library of Congress Cataloging in Publication Data

Stoken, Dick A
Cycles.

1. Business cycles.   2. Speculation.   I. Title.
HB3727.S8   338.5'4   77-20688
ISBN 0-07-061632-9

  234567890   KPKP   7654321098

The editors for this book were W. Hodson Mogan and Carolyn Nagy, the designer was Elliot Epstein, and the production supervisor was Teresa F. Leaden. It was set in Melior by University Graphics, Inc.

Printed and bound by The Kingsport Press

CYCLES

With love to
Antigone, Kingsley, André,
and their mother, Eva

CONTENTS

TO THE READER

We have now come full circle. During the late 1960s and early 1970s, the American people and their elected officials came to believe that the old economic theories and principles no longer applied. Government could now prevent recessions. Government could now promote prosperity at will. Government could now repeal the old economic laws. And government could at last put the nail on the coffin of the business cycle.

Ten years later, in the spring of 1978, we are wiser. The 1974–1975 recession, the combination of high inflation and high unemployment, and today's profitless "prosperity" are leading us back to the old economic principles which we once threw away so recklessly.

As we enter 1978, the condition of the economy gives little hope for a quick and easy respite. Once again, government is being viewed as more of a troublemaker than a helper. We are now faced with deflation in farm prices, disinflation in industrial prices, and inflation almost everywhere else. How can this be? Can't government solve our economic problems anymore? If it cannot, then let us explore economic history and previous cycles, and learn from them. An examination of the past clearly indicates that the excesses of the late 1960s and early 1970s must be corrected.

This book, as its title indicates, is about cycles. It points out their inevitability and tells us how to profit from them. There are cycles in all spheres of human endeavor, from stocks and bonds to commodities and political preferences. Human nature is never constant; it swings back and forth from one excess to another, from one cycle to another.

The book should be of interest to investors, business people, speculators, and students of human nature. Investors who were familiar with the principles herein would have avoided the terrific beating of the stock and bond markets during the 1966–1977 period. Business people who familiarized themselves with business cycle theory could have saved millions of dollars in inventory losses during the 1974–1975 period. Had they been reminded that shortages are a temporary phenomenon, at best, they might have cut back on inventories during 1974, rather than adding to them. The speculator will learn when to take the huge risks that promise the brass ring, and when to go fishing. The student of human nature will learn why there are cycles, and in doing so will, hopefully, understand the whys and wherefores of the human race a little better.

Acknowledgments

I would like to thank Eunice Rosen, Kiril Sokoloff, Dominick Abel, Haskell Benishay, Bennett Kremen, and Paul Henkel for reading the manuscript and making many helpful suggestions.

ONE

AN INTRODUCTION TO CYCLES

We are victims of a 54-year cycle of economic activity which goes from bust to boom to bust again. This long-term cycle has an important effect on all of us, as it influences the way we act in our social and political as well as our economic life. Had we been familiar with this cycle, the events of 1973–1974—a raging inflation, accompanied by increasing social unrest and a breakdown of authority, and followed by the most severe recession and stock market break in a generation—events which have occurred approximately every 54 years with surprising regularity, would have come as no surprise.[1] In fact, investors could have been out of the stock market during this debacle and yet, if they were so inclined, they could have taken advantage of the spectacular rise that was occurring in the price of commodities.

However, we live in an age which is skeptical about cycles, especially when their existence is explained as due to sun spots or other mysterious factors somewhere out there in the universe. In a world that believes in reason and the inevitability of progress, such explanations are seen as a throwback to more primitive times. And the cycles that we do acknowledge, such as the traditional four-year business cycle, are taken to be an aberration that we have not yet learned to control. They are not seen as inevitable.

But if we look around us we see all sorts of events that occur with

---

[1]The last huge inflation occurred in 1920.

regularity. There are seasons of the year, a cycle of life which goes from birth to old age and death, and a 28-day menstrual cycle. A whole school of history—whose leaders extend from Thucydides to Toynbee—claims that there is a cyclical pattern to history; that after coming into existence the important nation-states, from Greece and Rome of antiquity to Great Britain, the leader of the nineteenth century, grow and mature, and then decline and fall with a periodic regularity.

The reason for economic cycles is not mysterious but is rooted in the nature of the way people relate to their world. Just as our elaborate solar system is held together by a gravitational pull between the heavenly bodies, so there are sociobiological pulls between people and nature and between people and other people. We can see this by supposing a group of animals which feeds on one type of insect. So long as there are many of these insects, the animals have plenty of food and therefore multiply. Yet, as they continue to do so, the insects get pretty well eaten up, depleting the animals' source of food. The animals then begin dying off and their disappearance enables the insects to begin multiplying. Just when it looks as if these animals are about to become extinct, the insects become numerous, providing a source of food so that once more the animals can multiply. So, over a period of time, the animal population fluctuates from large to small to large.

Just as the animal population both affects and is affected by the population of the insects it feeds upon, so the desire to be a risk taker—as opposed to a risk averter—both affects and is affected by the ebbs and flows of the economy, that is, the alternating states of prosperity and depression. A risk taker is someone who attempts to benefit from a growing economy. While generally thought of as profit seekers, such as entrepreneurs and speculators, risk takers also include those who adopt a standard of living that does not leave much room for savings. Risk averters, on the other hand, are not willing to depend upon an expanding economy for their well-being. They include not only those who seek the security of a steady paycheck, such as salaried employees and bureaucrats, but also those who delay consumption so that they may build up the level of their savings. These two broad categories, with much overlapping and to differing degrees within individuals, describe a tendency either to extend or not to extend one's economic commitments.

What happens is that a period of prosperity leads people to believe their economic conditions will continue to improve. The desire to become a risk taker increases: entrepreneurs increase their economic commitments, people eat into their savings and increase their standard of living, and some risk averters become risk takers. These tendencies in turn fuel the broad economic expansion. However, as this economic trend continues, the desire to become a risk taker becomes unreasonably great. When too many of the participants attempt to become risk takers, we build supplies to the point where they become excessive in relation to demand, at the very time that business costs have become too high. Behavior must be altered so that at least some people become risk averters; that is, they stop borrowing money, stop building economic commitments, and increase their work effort. In order for this to happen, it is necessary for people to experience an economic setback. Thus, just as night follows day, contractions follow expansions.

We can see this inevitable sequence by looking at what happens during the traditional business cycle. Business people who are, in general, risk takers respond to deteriorating business conditions by reducing their economic goods—inventories, capital expenditures, etc.—and laying off workers. As these unemployed workers begin curtailing their expenditures, the contraction spreads. However, at some point, the inventory liquidation exceeds the falloff in sales—business executives find they have cut inventories too much. They then have to reverse course and begin increasing their stock of economic goods. As business costs (both capital and labor) have been reduced—due to the contraction there was a lessening in the demand for money, along with a weeding out of the least efficient workers, and thus a rise in labor productivity—this increase in the level of business activity is quickly reflected in increased profits.

The increased profits serve to restore the business executives' confidence, and the expansion is then underway. The business manager embarks on a policy of hiring more workers and building the company's capital stock—both inventories and capital goods. As paychecks fatten because of both a pickup in employment and overtime, confidence spills over to the workers, who increase their spending. This upswing spurs the business executive to greater levels of expansion. Yet, at some point, inventory accumulation surpasses the level of sales, and inventories and plant capacity become overbuilt. Retrenchment is then in order. As both capital and labor have become more costly—with the financing of these new and increased undertakings the demand for money has increased, and with the hiring of the less experienced workers labor productivity has decreased—this lessened volume of business activity is quickly reflected in lower earnings. Once again, business confidence is shaken, workers are laid off, and unemployment increases. This loss of confidence spreads to the consumer, who further curtails spending, thus adding to the contraction. The important thing is to recognize that it is *the changes in confidence. an intangible factor,* which, by affecting people's willingness to undertake economic risk, fuel these expansions and contractions along their way.

This same relationship between the desire to be a risk taker and the state of the economy also occurs over a larger spectrum, producing long economic cycles. Once there has been extended prosperity, people experience a lesson of pleasure. That is, the increase in the value of assets, job security, and the standard of living has well exceeded what people had expected. As a result, the world now appears less risky and this illusion induces a fundamental change in people's behavior. The dominant theme becomes the pursuit of pleasure or the extension of one's influence. In the economic sphere, people gain confidence, become optimistic in their expectations of future business conditions, and attempt to take advantage of the prosperity. The desire to become a risk taker increases. This desire leads people to begin increasing their economic commitments; they become entrepreneurs, acquire assets, take on debt, and increase their consumption.

These actions create an underlying source of support to the economy so that a contraction does not feed upon itself. Business managers who had been witnessing huge backlogs of orders and prospective business entrepreneurs both take advantage of the falloffs in the costs of capital and labor which occur during a contraction to

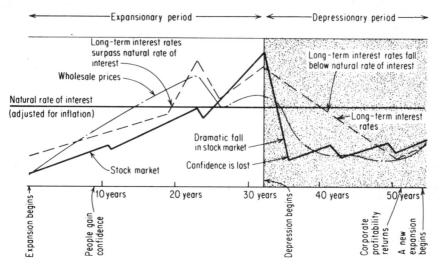

FIGURE 1   A LONG-TERM ECONOMIC CYCLE.

expand their capital investment. As their long-term expectations are now favorable, consumers do not cut their expenditures materially during these setbacks; rather, they dip into savings in order to maintain their standard of living. The result is that for a long period of time, business contractions are cut short or prevented from gaining momentum, while during each expansion business activity surpasses the levels achieved during the peak of the preceding expansion. And throughout this long period, which in this book we shall call the expansionary phase of the cycle, there is a growing demand for goods and credit, which leads to rising wholesale prices and rising long-term interest rates.

As the prosperity continues, however, the success of the economy and of those who have committed themselves to it is widely recognized. Large numbers of people now come to believe in the continuance of this trend, thinking what happened in the past will keep happening, and they attempt to become risk takers. An influx of new entrepreneurs attempting to exploit the promising investment opportunities, combined with an enormous increase in expenditures by consumers, leads to an increased demand for credit. The cost of capital (long-term interest rates) rises above the natural rate of interest (which is about 3½%),[2] adjusted for past inflation (which, if figured in 1967, was about 2%).

In paying more for money than the natural rate of interest, risk takers are committing an error of optimism. The reason is that their strong desire to become risk takers is, at the same time, also producing an explosion in the demand for raw materials, agricultural products, fuel, and labor, which outstrips their supply. As the prices of these goods are bid up, we get a soaring inflation, and as workers, feeling more secure about their economic prospects, become more prone to job-hopping, absenteeism, and strikes, we get a sharp fall in labor productivity. The cost of doing business mounts so that it becomes difficult for risk takers to earn the investment return that had been expected.[3] Corporate profitability is put in jeopardy and we get a sharp contraction.

However, as we have not overbuilt our supply of goods in relation to demand, or exhausted the profitable investment opportunities, this is not the end of the expansionary phase. Following a modest improvement in the cost of doing business, the army of risk takers continues to build its economic commitments. This leads to an increase in business activity, which in turn allows business people to raise prices and offset their high costs—long-term interest rates remain above the natural rate, indicating that costs are still high—for a while at least.

The profitable investment opportunities (the number of which is always limited) are soon exhausted and a proliferation of less profitable and more marginal ventures, along with a great deal of imitation within the more successful industries, follows. Yet, as this new investment, unlike investment initiated at the beginning of the expansionary phase, is undertaken at a time when costs are high, the conditions for a huge bust are now complete. The enormous

---

[2]The natural rate of interest is the supposed rate of return on capital (after inflation has been subtracted). Although economists have not been able to quantify this natural rate, if we average long-term interest rates, less an allowance for inflation, over a 150-year period, we get about 3½%.

[3]As labor and debtors (the lenders of capital) are getting a great share of the sales dollar, there is less available for a return on equity.

increases in spending for capital items have led to a great deal of excess capacity. And because of the financing of these projects, we get an excessive amount of debt together with a deterioration in its quality (due to the financing of the less profitable and marginal ventures). With markets in many areas becoming saturated, the pace of economic activity slackens so that business people can no longer raise prices to offset their increased costs. As profits begin to erode the excess capacity and excessive debt cannot be supported, they must be liquidated (see Figure 1).

Soon, a business contraction, in forcing people to reduce some of their excessive economic commitments, gains momentum and becomes a lesson of pain. People experience an unexpected falloff in the value of assets, job security, and their standard of living. The world begins to appear risky and this uncertainty induces a fundamental change in the way people act; they now attempt to avoid pain or protect themselves. In the economic sphere, people lose confidence, their expectations become pessimistic, and they attempt to become risk averters. When this change occurs, the underlying source of the long economic expansion is pulled away. Contractions are no longer met with new spending by business owners and an attempt by consumers to maintain their standard of living: thus, these contractions now feed on themselves. They are no longer pauses in a major expansion but parts of what in this book is called a depressionary phase. And this depressionary phase continues—with brief periods of expansion—until the desire to become a risk averter grows too widespread, that is, until most of the risk takers have become risk averters.

Consumers now postpone their purchases, while business executives either terminate their operations, or reduce debt, fire workers, and discontinue unprofitable ventures. This retrenchment results in a weeding out of excess capacity, a backlog of consumer demand, a buildup in the supply of credit as savings increase, and a backlog of promising investment ideas because of a lack of risk takers to develop them. As the demand for money lessens, long-term interest rates fall below the natural rate (adjusted for past inflation). This fall in the cost of capital to below the natural rate is now an error of pessimism. Here, the same reason, a lack of risk takers, leading to this fall in long-term interest rates is also producing a reduction in the demand for raw materials, agricultural products, and labor. This declining demand in turn leads to a huge fall in wholesale prices and a sharp rise in labor productivity (workers become willing to put in a full day's sweat for their paychecks). Business costs are dramatically lowered, so that new investment is now able to produce a favorable investment return. Then, after a few years, when business experiences a sharp rise in profits, the forces of expansion are set in motion once again.[4]

Without a knowledge of this long-term cycle, investors have difficulty understanding the importance of what is happening. They are like soldiers in one field of battle who, upon seeing the enemy retreat, think the war is being won, while in truth the decisive battle is being fought somewhere else and is being lost. However, by understanding this long-term cycle, investors become like generals on the hill, observing all the battles and thus being more likely to predict the outcome of the war. They no longer are likely to see 1968, when optimism in the economy ran rampant, as a safe time to buy stocks, or the stock market rally of August–October 1973 as the beginning of a new bull market. As Adam Smith said in *The Money Game,*[5] "You do have to know what time of market it is. Markets go in cycles like all the other rhythms of life."

During each cycle, there are typically five long bull markets wherein the value of stocks—and other assets—show a dramatic increase.[6] Since 1896, the beginning of the last cycle, (which ended in 1949) there have been seven such bull markets. In the course of this book, we shall show how these bull markets can be spotted. An investor who began in 1896 with this knowledge and $1000 would have amassed a portfolio (not including reinvestment of dividends) worth approximately $5.5 million by December 1976. This course of action corresponds to a $50,000 portfolio had this investor merely bought and held a representative list of stocks. In addition, by

---

[4]This long economic cycle, while similar to that described in the mid-1920s by the Russian economist Nikolai Kondratieff, is different in several important respects: The cycle presented in this book has different turning points; it is fueled by a changing human psychology, and, as we shall see later, is itself changing.

[5]New York: Random House, Inc., 1967.

[6]This is explained more fully in Chapter 7.

selling out at the end of each of these bull markets, this investor would have avoided the brunt of the seven bear markets (since 1900) wherein prices broke 40% or more from their highs. We are currently in the eighth bull market wherein the value of our assets should show a dramatic increase during the next five to seven years. As an expanding economy generates a higher level of profits, an increasing optimism is likely to replace the pessimism that followed the serious recession of 1973–1974. More and more people will then become drawn into the stock market and be willing to pay more for a given dollar of earnings.

Perhaps the best way to view a long economic cycle is to study the anatomy of one.

TWO

AN ANATOMY OF A CYCLE

In 1897, following a 24-year period of recurring depression, the United States economy began a 32-year period of prosperity. An inflation, which resulted from the expansion in money supply that followed the new gold discoveries in South Africa, and the Spanish-American War helped stimulate business to move out of the mire of depression. The stock market started a long rise which was to increase the Dow Jones Industrial Average by 1800% in 33 years. Moreover, long-term interest rates, along with wholesale prices, began a secular rise which, with brief interruptions, lasted 21 years (Chart 1).

This expansion commenced with the revival of the railroad industry, which for the past 40 years had been the dominant industry. The railroad, in leading to a vast expansion of markets, had been at the heart of our previous economic growth.

The first decade of this expansion was a period of conformity accompanied by social tranquillity. People were pleased with the way things were going—the inflation was easily cooled and the economy continued to expand—and did not want to rock the boat. The following two recessions were both mild, and confidence in the future of the economy began to return. Business profits now were fairly easy to come by: the earlier depression had left as its legacy a lowered cost of capital and labor, as well as reduced competition, which, in turn, made it easier to raise prices.

By 1906 the evidence of this growing prosperity had shown up

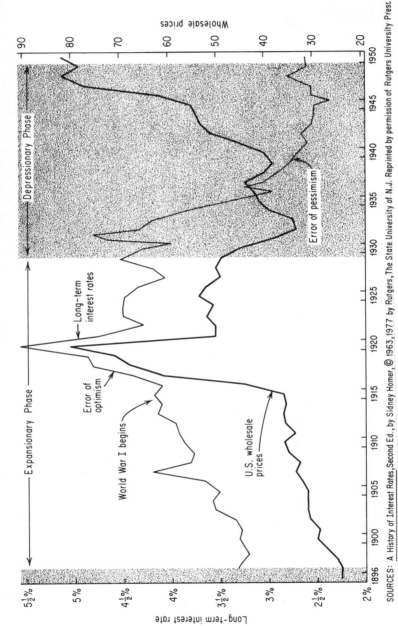

SOURCES: *A History of Interest Rates,* Second Ed., by Sidney Homer, © 1963, 1977 by Rutgers, The State University of N.J. Reprinted by permission of Rutgers University Press.

CHART 1 INTEREST RATES AND WHOLESALE PRICES, 1896 TO 1950. The error of optimism occurred in 1917 when interest rates got to 4½% (the natural rate of interest of 3½%, plus an inflation rate of 1%). The shaded area represents the depressionary period.

12

almost everywhere and people began to lose the caution bred by the depression. The stock exchanges were hit with a wave of speculation. Business firms stepped up their spending for inventories and capital items, and the resulting demand for credit put a strain on the banking system, sharply raising the cost of capital. The costs of capital, labor, and materials had begun to outpace the ability of business to raise prices—increased competition had put pressure on prices—leaving the economy temporarily overextended.

The result was the serious recession of 1907, accompanied by the worst stock market break since the last depression, which served to shake the emerging confidence. Yet, while this contraction was more serious than the previous two, it did not degenerate into a depression, as had happened in the early 1890s. The underlying business fundamentals were sound. The market for goods was not saturated, nor had any serious excess capacity developed. Once people had gotten the message to proceed a bit more cautiously, labor productivity rose and capital became more abundant and cheaper. The upward march in long-term interest rates was interrupted (Chart 1). The expansion was ready to resume.

The automobile emerged from this serious recession as the new dominant industry. By spawning a series of supporting industries from tires to oil, and by providing a new path to profits, it spurred economic growth just as the railroads had, some 50 years back. As the potential from the railroads had now been exploited, the age of the automobile began. The following years saw the building of more and more roads, the introduction of the filling station, the spread of our commercial centers, and consequently a continuously expanding market for autos. The innovational impetus to our expansion had been provided.[1]

As we emerged from the serious recession of 1907 without slipping into a depression, business executives increased their capital

---

[1]The idea that the investment booms following the revolutionary innovations of the cotton mill, the railroad, and the automobile produced a long period of prosperity followed by a creative destruction was first expounded by Joseph Schumpeter, who taught economics at Harvard from 1932 to 1950. He described the latter as a period of depression where the excesses that resulted from the overbuilding of these innovations were eliminated so that a new innovation could bloom and spur another prosperity.

expenditures and consumers increased their spending on both necessities and luxuries. The buildup in the value of financial assets was resumed, long-term interest rates began rising again, and the following two recessions were mild.

As confidence that the economy would provide a more secure economic future spread, a subtle shift in people's attitudes occurred. We now thought we had the answers and could solve our problems. In 1913, in answer to the too easy and irresponsible buildup of credit that was considered responsible for the collapse of 1907 as well as for depressions in the nineteenth century, we instituted the Federal Reserve Act. By giving control over money and credit conditions to a central banking authority, we thought that we could put an end to the chief culprit of depression.

Yet, soon we began to feel that we had greater control over our destiny than we actually did. This was our time of illusion. We lost our conservatism and tried things that normally we would not have dreamed of. At such times we are more likely to respond to some perceived threat from a foreign power and to be led into a major war, not just a skirmish like the Spanish-American War. It was in 1917 that the United States followed her friends, Britain and France, into World War I.

However taxing this war seemed emotionally, it produced a special buoyancy that was engendered by huge injections of money into the war effort and the bidding for scarce supplies of labor and goods. These activities caused even the most marginal and risky ventures to prosper. It suddenly became clear that the borrowers and risk takers had been running away with the profits, while, in reality, the savers or lenders had been left with the risk. A shift in the collective viewpoint occurred. Life now seemed easier, so why not take some risks? As the risk takers began to act, the tempo of business picked up, and even those who had been accustomed to a steady paycheck now came to believe in the prosperity. Expectations soared, consumer demand reached unprecedented levels, and the long-term rate of interest surpassed 4½% (the natural rate of interest, adjusted for inflation, which was about 1%). (See Chart 1.) This willingness of borrowers to pay more for money than the natural rate of interest (adjusted for past inflation) was the sign that expectations in the future of our economy and the consequent desire to be a risk taker were becoming too high. People were committing an error of optimism.

In such an atmosphere, there is a change in psychology which spreads over the whole of our social fabric. People see themselves as more powerful and develop the psychology of affluence, wherein the dominant theme in their behavior becomes the pursuit of pleasure; they seek to live the good life and have fun. As people no longer need to cooperate for the common good, individualism rises again. And with it comes an increase in assertiveness, egotism, and arrogance.

With our participation in World War I came a rapid change in our standards of conduct (in both morals and manners); the tempo picked up, the music became faster; and sexual mores loosened. As the war came to a close, we were into the "jazz age" with its hip flasks, cheek-to-cheek dancing, and bona fide sexual revolution— girls were engaging in what F. Scott Fitzgerald, the leading spokesman of that age, termed "petting parties." Soon a generation gap arose as the children of that age rebelled against their parents, whose attitudes had been molded during the last depression.

At the same time, women, feeling less need for protection and security, took off their corsets, bared their legs (hemlines rose), and became more independent and aggressive. Their cry for equality became louder. By 1920, women had gotten the vote and had started smoking in public.

When living requires less risk, people also believe they can solve social problems. Prohibition was legalized in an attempt to rid society of the abuses and wastes attributed to overindulgence. As demands for social change increase, traditional authorities and institutions come under attack. There is a dramatic increase in the level of civil disorder, ending the period of social tranquillity that has accompanied the earlier part of the expansion. All of us, it seems, are ready to have a go at "getting ours." A wave of increasing crime, violence, and strikes sends a shiver down the spine of the middle class. Following World War I, we saw the Ku Klux Klan spread to the North; a bomb (supposedly set by Bolsheviks or anarchists) exploded on Wall Street right across from the leading banking house, J. P. Morgan & Co., killing 30 people; and a multitude of unauthorized strikes were called against municipal governments.

In the economic sphere we got a raging inflation, particularly in commodities; by 1920 the price of silk rose to the unheard-of level of $18.40 per pound, while wheat went from $1 to $3.50 per bushel. There was a frenzy of speculative activity on the stock exchanges. Unlike the stimulative inflation that occurred at the beginning of the expansion, this latter stage of inflation was a sign that expectations had become too high and were interfering with producers' abilities to increase supplies, thus interrupting the broad economic expansion. As it became more profitable to try to outguess the inflation than to engage in productive efforts, business people began to speculate in commodities rather than to produce them, so that the economic game became a money game. Money that normally flowed into productive channels was now used to finance the inflation. With the risk takers now getting a giant slice of the pie, the relationship between effort and reward was undermined and the work ethic was dulled, thus leading to a sharp decline in productivity. With business costs exceeding the ability of business to raise prices, the economy was again overextended, only this time more seriously so than in 1906. Moreover, because of these high costs, potential areas of new growth could not be developed.

Almost overnight, we plummeted into a serious recession, accompanied by the worst stock market break in over 35 years. With President Wilson incapacitated by a stroke suffered while taking his case for the League of Nations to the people, we lost faith in the government's ability to handle economic problems. Confidence was severely shaken. Unemployment rose to the highest levels since the depression of the 1890s, and amidst a widespread cancellation of orders, a sweeping deflation began (by late 1921 the price of silk had broken to $5.80 per pound and wheat had dropped to $1 per bushel), baring the possibility of a real collapse. The prophets of doom surfaced to tell us of the depression that awaited us just around the corner.

Yet, too many people were committed to the economy to let the deflation run its natural course. As if by an unspoken agreement, the leaders—bankers, big business, and big government—rallied to the rescue of the economy. The Federal Reserve began loosening credit in 1921, while some of the leading corporations came to the aid of their ailing brethren, such as Du Pont's bailout of General Motors.[2] The system shuddered a bit but stayed intact. As the profitable investment opportunities had not been exploited as yet, nor had our productive facilities been overbuilt, the economy could be propped up before a depression had set in.

As life did not appear quite so easy, people became less inclined to undertake economic risks; consumers curtailed their spending and business executives became more cautious. Both long-term interest rates and wholesale prices fell, lowering business costs. In general, the heightened economic expectations of the past few years were cooled.

As the worst did not happen and as the economy, once again, began expanding, we regained our confidence. With it came a new maturity. We were tired of social experiments and were no longer about to follow anyone who promised to lead us to the cherished land. Instead, we yearned to restore the old values. In a nutshell, we became more conservative both politically and economically. An obscure senator from Ohio, Warren G. Harding, campaigned for the Presidency in 1920 on the promise of a "return to normalcy."

The stock market resumed its upward course, and social tensions eased. The following recession, in 1923, was mild, and once again we seemed to be solving our problems. In late 1927, after yet another mild recession, Lindbergh captured the imagination of the masses by flying the Atlantic Ocean nonstop. This act of inspiration served to set expectations rising much too fast. Business leaders and workers once again began losing their caution.

The period of 1927 to 1929 was one of excessive overoptimism. Economic commitments were pushed too far and stretched too thin. An orgy of speculation unlike anything seen before or since hit our stock exchanges. Brokerage offices were jammed with crowds of people, including shoeshine boys, seamstresses, and chauffeurs, who were willing to pay almost any price to participate in the bull market. In the 18-month period from March 3, 1928, to September 3, 1929, Montgomery Ward went from $133 to $466; Westinghouse

---

[2]In 1921, Du Pont arranged for J. P. Morgan & Co. to provide financing to a troubled General Motors.

from $92 to $313, and RCA, the darling of this bull market, from $95 to $505.[3] (During the same period, the Dow Jones Industrial Average itself rose from 191 to 381!)

Yet, this speculative fever was by no means confined to the stock market. Many of the business minds of the nation were diverted to speculative activity—to increasing their business inventories and pursuing other marginal ventures. As more and more risk takers appeared on the scene, there was a proliferation of imitators, financial manipulators, and fast-buck artists all seeking easy riches. With this fever came a deterioration in the quality of bank loans. As the more promising of the new investment ideas were exploited, we got more and more imitation. The more profitable an investment is, the larger the number of people who want to get into it. The automobile and its supporting industries began growing by leaps and bounds. By 1929, there were 27 million motor vehicles on American roads as against 10½ million in 1921, and the automobile industry accounted for more than a tenth of the value of all manufactured goods. Finally, other nations joined in the prosperity, building up their productive factors and thus taking markets away from the United States. Consequently, when long-term interest rates, and hence business costs, began to rise, once again the economy became overextended.

However, this overextension was not—as in 1906 or 1920—a temporary phenomenon. The reason was that the serious contraction of 1920 did not go far enough in correcting the problems that had built up in the earlier part of the expansion. While long-term interest rates had fallen, they still remained above the natural rate of interest; labor productivity had improved, but not to the level prevailing at the beginning of the expansionary period; and economic expectations, while cooled, were still high by past standards. The grossest excesses were liquidated, but that was all. Thus, the 1920s, while they appeared prosperous, were built on a foundation of sand. They began with a relatively high cost of capital, low labor productivity, and a high desire for risk taking, when compared with what existed in 1897. The result was that the new investment during the following years took place at a high level of fixed cost, so that corporate profitability was put in jeopardy. As we continued to build our

---

[3]These prices are adjusted for splits.

productive facilities and take on debt at this high cost, and while consumer demand was not increasing at the rate business executives had been expecting, the economy became severely overextended and this strain could not be patched up.

In late 1929, the economy weakened, and as it failed to meet expectations, confidence was undermined. The gates were opened for a massive liquidation. The stock market began falling, and within a period of 10 weeks the Dow Jones Industrial Average had given up 50% of its entire 33-year advance. As problems that were formerly pushed under the rug started popping out, recoveries were aborted, and this contraction snowballed into a depression.

Blaming the depth of the Great Depression on some special event, such as Britain's going off the gold standard in 1931, is putting the cart before the horse. During these times, things people had not bargained for came to light. Walter Bagehot, a financial chronicler of nineteenth-century England, wrote: "Every great crisis reveals the excessive speculation of many houses which no one before suspected." As the various nations' domestic economies experienced breakdown, people became concerned with protecting their own economies and thus were no longer willing to make the accommodations necessary for the maintenance of the international monetary and trade system: The international system broke down and the depression became worldwide in the early 1930s.

The depressionary phase of the cycle began with the depression of 1929–1933. What in 1907 and 1920–1921 had been merely a crisis of confidence had now turned into a mass loss of confidence wherein the hopes and illusions of all who had believed in the prosperity were shattered. Long-term interest rates and wholesale prices declined; unemployment mounted, business earnings fell, bankruptcies abounded, and business appeared to come to a standstill. A great number of people who had witnessed a continued expansion in the value of their capital assets were faced with a catastrophic fall in their value. From common stocks and real estate to antiques and art objects, nothing survived this massive downward readjustment in values. The Dow Jones Industrial Average fell 89% from its 1929 high. Westhinghouse fell to $16, RCA to $18, and Montgomery Ward hit a price of $4. The arrogance and overconfidence of this age were now washed away.

The political party in office was held responsible for this awful debacle and was thrown out. With the election of Franklin D. Roosevelt, a 72-year reign of the Republican Party, wherein the Democrats were able to hold the White House for only 16 years and never for more than 8 years consecutively, came to an end. The Democrats became the new majority party. And we began a long period wherein the Republicans could never hold the White House for more than 8 consecutive years.

Finally, the liquidation temporarily went too far. Both stock and commodity prices soon experienced a sharp rebound from their depression lows; business earnings began increasing, and a broad recovery seemed to be in process. As this business expansion continued, hopes began rising that the former value of our assets would soon be restored. However, the liquidation of 1929–1933, while severe, was not complete. Excess capacity was not completely liquidated; debt liquidation had not run its full course and business costs, while lower, were not dramatically lower. Thus, at this time, the attempt to rebuild inventories and undertake capital expenditures was too much for the economy to handle.

Another contraction soon began, and it set off a second wave of liquidation which dashed the hopes that were beginning to emerge during the business recovery. This second contraction, while not so severe as the previous one, was also an economic contraction of major proportions. Once again, the price of stocks and commodities broke sharply. The period from 1929 through the second depression, which ended in 1938, *was the heart of the depressionary phase.*

As there were widespread misery and discontent, social strife again surfaced. Only this time labor was in the forefront, demanding protection from the depression. The period also brought a rash of particularly bloody mass-organizing strikes by the Congress of Industrial Organizations (CIO) and a march on Washington by the Bonus Army of 15,000 unemployed veterans of World War I who hoped to persuade Congress that their bonus certificates should be paid immediately.

The dominant industry, the automobile, was hit with an epidemic of bankruptcies as the weak sisters were weeded out and excess capacity was brought down. The railroads, which had outserved their usefulness by this time, found themselves in serious trouble. And the long-term rate of interest fell below the natural rate (adjusted for inflation), signaling that economic expectations had fallen and consequently the desire to become a risk averter was becoming strong. People were now committing an error of pessimism.

Naturally, because of the seriousness of the depression, business now got the support of government in protecting its domestic markets. Congress passed the Smoot-Hawley bill, raising tariffs. The search for the cause of this depression began and soon focused on Keynes's diagnosis of insufficient demand. This diagnosis eventually led to the passage of the Full Employment Act in 1946 whereby the government assumed responsibility to maintain full employment. And, in order to help ease the pain of depression, broad-scale reforms were undertaken. In this case, the New Deal offered humanitarian solace to millions of Americans and we began the welfare state.

Following the heart of the depression, a gradual improvement in business began and soon spread to the stock market. However, even though much of the excess capacity and debt had been liquidated, when hopes were again shattered following the last recovery, a widespread disillusionment had set in. As the depression undermined the financial assets, job security, career objectives, and the ability to cope financially, people's ideas of risk changed. They saw themselves as less powerful and adopted the psychology of deflation wherein the dominant theme became the achievement of security and self-protection against whatever lay ahead. A fundamental change in people's attitudes occurred as they became more trusting, more accommodating, and more willing to accept an authority that would provide some direction. In the economic sphere, people grew more guarded and cautious and less inclined to take a risk.

Because of the widespread pessimism, people did not believe the real improvement that was developing in many sectors of the economy, and they kept looking over their shoulders for a recurrence of the depression. The psychological measures, such as stock prices and interest rates, seemed not to reflect the extent of this real improvement, and people regarded the greater activity in business as largely a consequence of World War II.[4] So, when it became apparent that peace was at hand in 1945, these people reduced their spending, and we got another contraction followed by a sharp stock market break.

This contraction once again destroyed the emerging confidence and cast a pall over business, so the following recovery was cut short and by 1948 we got another recession. Yet, as these two contractions were less severe than the preceding ones, people began to loosen their purse strings. As business costs had been reduced through the cost of capital having become cheap and the return of the work ethic having brought about a dramatic improvement in labor productivity, a fundamental improvement in business conditions had taken place. New investment could now be undertaken at a low level of fixed cost. By 1949, one complete cycle had come to an end and we were ready to begin another period of prosperity.

The same experience of a long period of prosperity followed by a period of depression also occurred in England during the nineteenth century. Britain's example can be especially useful because at that time England was the major source of finance and advanced technology, just as the United States is today.

We find striking similarities between the expansion of 1897–1929 in the United States and the expansions of 1785–1815 and 1843–1873 in England (see Table 2-1). The invention of the cotton mill provided the innovational impetus for the expansion of 1785–1815, just as the automobile was to do for the United States expansion of 1897–1929. As England had not yet ascended to economic leadership, the stimulative inflation began in France (the leading country at that time).[5] A tripling of the French government's debt in the 15

---

[4]This major war, unlike the others during the last 200 years, occurred during a depressionary period, rather than during an expansionary period. We shall go into this more fully later.

[5]An earlier attempt at an economic takeoff by France had collapsed in the aftermath of the John Law debacle where unsuspecting French investors were sold shares in a company which owned unsettled land around our Mississippi River at increasingly exorbitant prices. However, it seems that a certain semblance of economic prosperity continued, residing mostly in the upper levels of society. This appearance of well-being may have allowed France to remain the dominant economic power until the end of the eighteenth century.

TABLE 2-1

Supercycles	Expansion-ary phase	Peak expec-tations	Over-abundance	Depression-ary period	Heart of depression-ary period
ENGLAND					
1785–1843	1785–1815	1803	1803–1815	1815–1843	1815–1832
1843–1897	1843–1873	1866	1867–1873	1873–1897	1873–1885
UNITED STATES					
1897–1949	1897–1929	1920	1921–1929	1929–1949	1929–1938

From the end of the heart of the depressionary period in one cycle to the same point in the next cycle was 53 years in both cases; and from the heart of the depression in one cycle to peak expectations in the following cycle was 34 years and 35 years, respectively.

years prior to the French Revolution had a vast inflationary impact on England, then conducting a major part of her trade with France.

During the following years, business activity rose briskly and setbacks were relatively mild. Soon, England's confidence grew and she rose to the growing threat that France presented to her markets. Britain's war with France acted as a stimulus to business and led to an enormous inflation, the sign that too many demands were being placed on the economy. There was social unrest, characterized by the Luddites, workers in England who rebelled against machines by destroying them, and the first call for women's equality was issued during this time. In 1792, Mary Wollstonecraft published "Vindication of the Rights of Woman," a treatise that called for equal rights and equal opportunities for all human beings irrespective of their sex.

Following a serious economic contraction which began in 1802 and was accompanied by falling commodity prices and long-term interest rates, British expectations were cooled. However, just as the automobile industry was overbuilt during the 1920s, so, as prosperity resumed, there was an overbuilding of the cotton mills which culminated in the massive liquidation of 1815–1819.

The expansion of 1843–1873 began with the revival of the cotton industry. The Californian and Australian gold discoveries led to a stimulative inflation, which was soon cooled. As prosperity spread, the value of assets began a 30-year climb. The early years of this prosperity—until the 1860s—were a time of social tranquillity. The railroad soon blossomed out, replacing cotton (then becoming an older industry) as the leading industry and spawning a host of industries (such as iron and coal) to support it. Business recessions were mild until 1857, at which time confidence was shaken by a contraction more severe than those immediately preceding it, though not so severe as those during the prior depressionary period.

During this expansion, England did not become directly involved in a major war. However, the American South, which was both economically and politically close to England by virtue of producing seven-eighths of the world's cotton, became involved in a major conflict. The South attempted to break her ties to the Union at the risk of war. The result was the Civil War, which led to a surge of business vitality in England as lost markets had to be replaced and as Confederate capital sought refuge there.

The inflationary impact of the American Civil War provided the stimulus to heighten England's expectations, and a frenzy of speculative activity followed. Soon the economy became temporarily overextended, and in 1866 Britain suffered another serious recession wherein confidence was shaken. It began on May 11, 1866, Black Friday in England, as Overend, Gurney and Company failed. According to the *London Times*, the shock could be felt in the "remotest corners of the Kingdom" and "panic . . . swayed the City to and fro." However, the government soon suspended the Bank Charter Act, so that the Bank of England did not have to maintain its statutory reserves. This liquidation, as in 1920–1921 in America, did not snowball. Yet, expectations were cooled, confidence was restored, and there was a resurgence of economic vitality, just as we saw occurring in the United States following the serious contraction of 1920–1921.

The social unrest of this period resulted in the beginnings of the trade union movement. Also, Darwin's theory of evolution came into vogue at this time, providing the ammunition for a full-scale attack on traditional religion. With the appearance of John Stuart Mill's work "The Subjection of Women" in 1869, feminism was again

surfacing. Women were soon displaying a degree of self-assertive-
ness unusual for the time. And a wide range of new careers, from
nursing to school teaching to secretarial and sales work, were
opened up to women.

Just as Lindbergh's nonstop flight over the Atlantic later captured
the imagination of the masses, the opening of the Suez Canal in 1869
served as Britain's act of inspiration. The year 1869 also marked the
completion of the first American transcontinental railroad, an
accomplishment that inspired worldwide confidence. In the following four years, there was furious industrial activity and a frenetic
period of overbuilding on the railroads. Twenty-four thousand miles
of railroad were built in the United States, much of it financed by
British capital. During this time, credit was extended loosely without proper regard for the economic and financial soundness of the
venture. Finally, as her foreign competitors began eating into her
markets, Britain's economy became overburdened. By 1873, once
again, an overbuilt economy was ready to crumble. The collapse in
that year ushered in a long depressionary period.

We can now see that there were three long periods of expansion,
each of which was generally recognized as a time of prosperity,
wherein business contractions were not severe. The most important
similarity, however, was the long secular rise in long-term interest
rates[6] to above the natural rate of interest (adjusted for inflation)
which was about 5% during Britain's first expansionary period (1½%
inflation assumed) and 3½% during her second expansionary period
(no inflation). This was the sign that people were committing an
error of optimism and that the groundwork was being laid for
another period of depression. Following the break in these long-term
interest rates during the second serious contraction of this expansionary period, interest rates stabilized at a level not far below their
peaks. Thus, the cost of new investment remained high, putting a
crimp into business profits. Within a relatively short period of time,
this led to a depression (Chart 2).

There are also remarkable similarities between the depressionary
period of 1929–1949 in the United States and the depressionary

------

[6]Wholesale prices also rose during the same period.

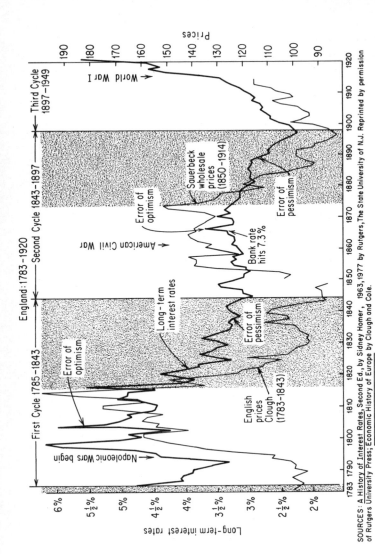

England: 1783-1920

SOURCES: A History of Interest Rates, Second Ed., by Sidney Homer, 1963, 1977 by Rutgers, The State University of N.J. Reprinted by permission of Rutgers University Press; Economic History of Europe by Clough and Cole.

CHART 2 INTEREST RATES AND WHOLESALE PRICES, ENGLAND, 1783–1920. The error of optimism occurred in about 1803 when the rate of interest hit 5% (based on 1½% inflation), 1864 when the rate of interest got to 3½% (based on no inflation—in this case, short-term rates were up sharply, the bank rate averaged 7.3% in 1864, the highest of the century), and 1917 when the rate of interest reached 4½%. The sharp rise in the rate of interest at the beginning of the first two expansionary phases (1797 and 1848) were associated with the stimulative inflations. The shaded areas represent the depressionary periods.

periods of 1815–1843 and 1873–1897 in England. The period of 1815–1843 began with the massive liquidation of 1815–1819, which brought about falling commodity prices, falling long-term interest rates, and rising unemployment. After a partial recovery from the depths of depression, similar to what was to occur in the United States in the early 1930s, a second contraction of major proportions began in 1825 and lasted until 1832. This period from 1815 through 1832 was the heart of this depressionary period and was followed by a gradual improvement in business which aborted in 1837 with a further wave of liquidation.

During this period, the inefficient and technically obsolescent enterprises were weeded out—especially in the cotton industry. The search for a culprit this time zeroed in on restrictive trade and the high price of food stuffs. In the 1840s, in an attempt to stimulate free trade, the English repealed the Corn Laws; duties on foreign grains were, for all practical purposes, eliminated. Free trade became a basic economic tenet to be held with a religious conviction by the ordinary Britisher, just as the idea that the government should be responsible for maintaining a healthy, expanding economy is almost a commandment among a majority of Americans today.

Also, during this time, there was a changing of the guard. The new Liberal Party, which was to dominate English politics for over 50 years, achieved power, just as the Democratic Party was to do in the United States during the 1930s. Furthermore, the attempt to increase the voting franchise and free people from the restrictions of a precapitalistic society resulted in the passage of the reform laws and the poor laws—the reforms of the period.

The period 1873–1897 began with the massive liquidation of 1873–1879. In fact, in British history this is referred to as the great depression. The heart of this depressionary period extended to 1886 and was followed by a gradual improvement in business which aborted in about 1892 with a further wave of liquidation.

During this depressionary period, the excesses of the prior expansion were liquidated. A surge of bankruptcies hit the railroads; the textile (or cotton) industry, the dominant industry of the earlier expansion, was especially hard hit; and just as we were to see in the United States during the 1930s, there was a drastic fall in the value of assets. Social strife surfaced with serious rioting in London and a violent miners' strike.[7]

The idea of free trade was challenged[8]; the dominance of the Liberal Party was broken; and the reforms of the period focused on unions and factory safety, or protecting the individual. The culprit of this depression was considered to be the British failure to increase her export markets. Consequently, the latter part of the nineteenth century saw Britain pursuing an aggressive policy of imperialism.

Each of these depressionary periods was widely recognized as a time of economic hardship, high levels of unemployment, and worldwide depression. Only four business contractions, either here or in England, in the past 130 years have lasted three years or longer, and each of these contractions came during the depressionary periods. Three occurred during the 1873–1897 period (1873–1879, 1882–1885, and 1892–1896 in England) and one (1929–1933) during the 1929–1949 depressionary period in the United States. And it was only during the depressionary periods, when confidence was lost, that the stock market was able to fall more than 50% from its highs. This drop occurred three times (since we have kept records): first in the 1870s, then in 1929–1933, and finally, from 1937 to 1942. But the most significant similarity and undeniable sign of bad times was the decline in long-term interest rates—lasting throughout the depressionary period—to well below the natural rate of interest (adjusted for inflation), signaling that the vast majority of people were now desiring to be risk averters and were thus committing an error of pessimism.[9] (See Charts 1 and 2.)

Thus, by 1949, we had three complete cycles of economic activity, from bust to boom to bust again. Each cycle began with a stimulative

---

[7]In the United States during the 1890s, we experienced a rash of bloody strikes (the Haymarket riots; Homestead, a branch of Carnegie Steel; and Pullman) which resulted in many deaths and a march on Washington by Coxey's Army (a march of the unemployed led by General Coxey of Ohio), to call attention to the suffering of labor during the depression.

[8]Lord Randolph Churchill sponsored a "Fair Trade League" in an attempt to institute moderate tariffs. Also, in an effort to appease the "protectionists," Great Britain did prohibit the importation of foreign livestock.

[9]Wholesale prices also fell through at least the heart of the depressionary period.

inflation along with the revival of the dominant industry. A new innovative industry soon blossomed to replace the older dominant industry. People slowly brought their expectations in line with the now affluent economy. And the resulting increase in confidence led to a war and a great deal of social unrest. The economy became temporarily overextended twice during the course of these expansions. The second of these overextensions was a result of the soaring inflation that followed the war. As the cost of capital and labor escalated, the promising new investment opportunities could not be developed. A serious contraction which interrupted the rise in the value of our financial assets followed. The risk takers took advantage of the moderate falloff in the cost of capital and labor that accompanied this contraction and developed the profitable investment opportunities. Finally, as too many people attempted to become risk takers and to undertake economic ventures, we developed a great deal of excess capacity along with a high cost of doing business, which led to a long period of depression.

During this time, we had three waves of liquidation or serious contractions, accompanied by a huge fall in the value of financial assets. There was a search for the culprit and an attempt at widespread reform. Finally, as the great majority of people became risk averters, the excess capacity developed during the prior expansion was worked off, a dramatic fall in business costs occurred, and a pent-up demand was built up. These occurrences, then, paved the way for the return of prosperity.

Does the period since 1949 conform to this cycle, or has the passage of the Full Employment Act, unlike the repeal of the Corn Laws 100 years ago, changed things? We will answer this question in the next chapter.

THREE

THE PRESENT CYCLE

In 1949, the United States economy emerged from a 20-year depression wherein the excesses of the last expansion had been worked off, and a long period of prosperity began. An expansion in money supply resulting from the financing of two wars—World War II and Korea—led to an inflation which, in turn, set the forces of expansion in motion. The automobile industry, the dominant industry, was revived, the stock market started a long advance, and long-term interest rates began a secular rise[1] (see Chart 3).

The 1950s were a period of conservatism. In retrospect, they were dull but good years, wherein we were pleased with the way things were going. The stimulative inflation was easily cooled; the following two recessions were relatively mild; and we had a period of social tranquillity such as had occurred at the beginning of the century. This tranquillity results because the social unrest accompanying a depression, unlike that which arises during an expansion, is alleviated by prosperity. Also, with the passage of the Full Employment Act of 1946, whereby the government assumed responsibility to maintain full employment, we felt that we now had a safeguard to protect the economy.

By 1959 confidence in the economy was beginning to spread. A wave of speculative activity, directed mostly into new issues, hit the stock exchanges. And as businesses stepped up their spending,

---

[1]Wholesale prices, which had bottomed in 1939, continued their rise.

31

United States 1949-1977

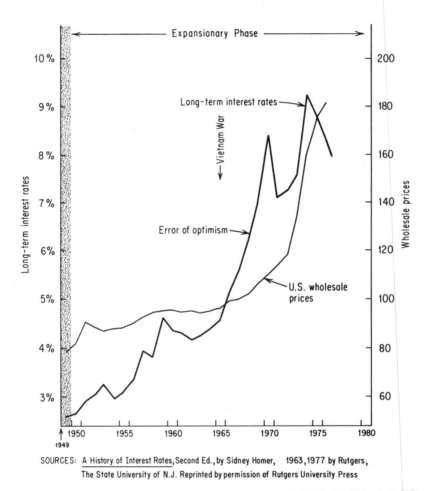

SOURCES: A History of Interest Rates, Second Ed., by Sidney Homer, 1963, 1977 by Rutgers, The State University of N.J. Reprinted by permission of Rutgers University Press

CHART 3 INTEREST RATES AND WHOLESALE PRICES, FROM 1949 TO 1977. The error of optimism occurred in about 1968, when interest rates surpassed 5½% (assumed a 2% inflation rate).

the cost of capital rose sharply. Business became temporarily overextended.

The result was the business recession of 1960–1961. Although this recession was not so severe as that of 1958 in terms of unemployment or falloff in industrial activity, it had a bigger impact on the psychological indicators, such as interest rates and stock prices. The broad rise in long-term interest rates was interrupted as these rates fell over a three-year period. And when President Kennedy attempted to roll back steel prices in 1962, just as we were emerging from the recession, the stock market suffered its worst break in 25 years. The result was that this recession, along with the sharp stock market break that followed, served to shake the emerging confidence, just as the serious recession of 1907 had.

However, as the underlying business conditions were sound, the economy did not turn down into a depression. Once people got the message to proceed more cautiously, speculative activity and some other excesses disappeared; the government passed the Investment Tax Credit Act and proposed an income tax cut; and there was a resurgence of economic vitality.

As we recovered from this recession, the computer emerged as the innovational leader spawning a host of supporting industries, such as transistors and data communications, and providing a new path to profits. The following years saw a revolution in the way of doing business and an ever expanding market for computers as banks, hospitals, brokerage firms, merchandisers, and others joined in the computer revolution. The age of the automobile gave way to the age of the computer.

As the expansion resumed, business owners increased their capital expenditures and consumers increased their spending. The buildup in the value of our financial assets continued. Long-term interest rates resumed their upward march, and the following recession, that of 1967, was mild.[2]

The improved economy led once more to a time of illusion wherein we believed we had the ability to solve our problems, right all the wrongs, and impose a better world. We entered into Vietnam, a taxing and emotional war, in 1965, and the consequent war effort sent our economy skyrocketing. The stock market became a scene of frantic speculative activity unlike anything seen since 1929. The

---

[2]This contraction was commonly called a growth recession. As long as there is a falloff in business spending as seen in the gross private domestic investment sector of the gross national product (GNP), along with a falloff in business earnings as seen in the Dow Jones Industrial Average, we can assume a contraction of sorts has occurred.

back offices of brokerage firms could not keep up with the heavy volume of trading. And, as small private companies were bought out at ridiculously high prices, new multimillionaires were created almost overnight.

We thought we were on the brink of perpetual prosperity. Walter Heller, who had been President Kennedy's chief economic adviser, said, "Gone is the countercyclical syndrome of the 1950s." Expectations soared; long-term interest rates exceeded 5½% (the natural rate of interest, adjusted for an assumed 2% inflation rate), signaling that people were committing an error of optimism again, as they had done 50 years before.

Once again, people developed the psychology of affluence wherein the dominant theme in their behavior became the pursuit of pleasure. An attitudinal change, based on a world that appeared less risky, spread throughout our social and political fabric. There was a rapid change in our manners and morals. The music became louder, and sexual mores loosened. The sexual revolution this time went well beyond one of F. Scott Fitzgerald's heroines' shocking confession that "I've kissed dozens of men, I suppose I'll kiss dozens more." The idea that we could be liberated from those economic chains which in the past had kept us from achieving personal fulfillment once again got a ready response. The women's liberation movement, seeking reforms in many areas, emerged. (During each expansionary period, women push their fight for equality at about this time.) And, as the demands for social change increased, we waged war on the home front against poverty and racial injustice.

Again, we developed a generation gap along with a challenge to authority which rocked the very institutions on which our social system rests. A wave of increased crime, assassinations, and terrorism brought an end to our long period of social tranquillity. Terrorist groups, such as the Weathermen or the Symbionese Liberation Army (SLA), flourished, along with an almost daily occurrence of bombings and skyjackings.

Following the relatively mild recession in 1970, a surge in consumer demand led to a raging inflation, particularly in commodities. The price of copper went from $.50 to $1.50 per pound, soybeans from $3.50 to $12.90 per bushel, and sugar, starting at 5¢, hit the unlikely price of 66¢ per pound. As it became easier to make money with the use of capital, money was drawn away from productive economic functions in order to finance speculative ventures. Also, as the work ethic was dulled, labor turnover, absenteeism, and strikes increased sharply. The resulting high costs impeded business profitability so that, by 1973, the economy was once again overextended.

When the inventory building had run its course, a widespread cancellation of orders led to a serious recession along with the worst stock market break in 35 years. Moreover, as Watergate surfaced to impede whatever ability the current administration might have had to deal with the inflation, confidence was shaken—only this time more seriously than in 1962. When unemployment rose to the highest levels since the last depression and a deflation set in, with the price of most commodities tumbling down (by 1975 copper hit $.50 a pound, soybeans sold at $4.50, and sugar at 8¢ a pound), the possibility of a real collapse was bared. The Cassandras appeared— only now they told of a hyperinflation and the imminent fall of our government.

However, just as they did in 1921, the leaders came to the aid of the economy. Taxes were cut, foreign loans—to Italy and Great Britain—were arranged, New York City was bailed out. With life again appearing not quite so easy, expectations fell, savings increased, and long-term interest rates broke, lowering business costs somewhat. As the profitable investment opportunities had not as yet been exploited or our productive facilities overbuilt, we were able to patch the economy before a depression set in.

The worst did not happen (New York City did not go bankrupt, Italy did not fall, and instead of slipping into a depression, business revived), and slowly we started to regain our confidence. The stock market began to rally. We became more conservative and less concerned about grand schemes, both social and political. Like Harding before him, Jimmy Carter, an obscure southern governor, gained the White House by dodging the issues and promising to restore the old and maligned values of trust in government and faith in our system. His inaugural speech, stating that "more is not necessarily better. . . . We cannot afford to do everything," reflected the new mood of the country. This is where we are now!—just entering the final part of our expansionary period.

This expansion, like past expansions, was accompanied, until its second serious recession, by rising long-term interest rates and wholesale prices. In 1974, right on schedule, 36 years after the heart of the depression,[3] we got a raging inflation followed by the worst recession and stock market break since the last depression. This cluster of events has occurred approximately every 54 years (see Table 2-1).

The evidence suggests that we are well into the fourth long-term economic expansion of the industrial revolution. In this case, the next five to seven years are likely to see a less activist society; a fading of the problems which plagued us in the late sixties and early seventies; and a return of political stability together with a fiscal and social conservatism. And, most important, *this is likely to be a time of noninflationary economic growth*—the next recession should be mild—accompanied by a broad bull market in stocks. The Dow Jones Industrial Average, if it is to equal the rise of 1800% which occurred during the last expansionary period, should sell at 2700. On the other hand, a fairly conservative objective, say a rise one-half as much as that in the prior expansionary period or a 900% rise, would still see the DJIA reach 1600.

However, these years of prosperity are likely to be built on a foundation of sand. The serious recession of 1973–1975 did not solve the problems that arose during the long expansion. The economy was propped up before the deflation was allowed to run its natural course. While business costs had fallen and debt had decreased, they were still high by past standards. In general, the excesses had not been eliminated. We began this portion of the expansion with the cost of capital and labor still high and the desire to be a risk taker still too strong. So, by about 1983–1985, it is likely that we will once again have overbuilt our key industries (the computer and its supporting industries); the profitable investment opportunities will probably have been exhausted; the underdeveloped countries will probably be unable to meet the excessive debt obligation they have incurred; and signs of overoptimism will most likely have appeared in the stock market. We will then be ready for a

---

[3]The heart of the last depressionary phase ended in 1938; 1920 came 35 years after the heart of the prior depressionary phase (which occurred in 1885); 1866 was 34 years after the heart of its prior depressionary phase (which came in 1832).

huge bust or *a genuine depression*, such as the one Great Britain experienced in the 1870s.

During the next depressionary period, we are likely to see a sharp fall in the value of our financial assets, falling wholesale prices, decreasing interest rates, along with a huge falloff in corporate earnings. The weak sisters of the computer industry should be weeded out, our dependence on the automobile is likely to be drastically curtailed, and the Democratic Party's period of ascendancy will most likely come to an end. We will no longer be able to sweep the excesses of the past expansion under the rug. The problems of our cities (such as New York) and troubled industries (such as railroads and utilities) will have to be dealt with.

As expectations are lowered, we are likely again to develop the psychology of deflation, wherein the dominant theme in our behavior becomes avoidance of pain. As a more cautious attitude takes root, we will be willing to settle for less—our emphasis will shift to security and cooperation. In all probability, women will lower their skirts (or hemlines, if you prefer), tighten their morals, and look to men to provide protection, shelter, and support. The various social causes which sprang to life during the sixties and seventies are likely to be replaced by a coalescence—with labor in the forefront— behind a new cause, that is, the elimination of the culprit responsible for the depression. In this atmosphere, the idea that the government should be responsible for our economic security is likely to be pushed further, leading to greater government involvement in our economy.

This depressionary period may very well be less severe or bloody than that of the thirties, however. The reason is that during a country's tenure as innovational and financial leader of the world, her economy proceeds to higher levels of adaptability and she puts into effect mechanisms to cushion a depression.

Britain began her tenure of economic leadership, which was to last for just under three cycles, or two and a half, to be exact, by beginning the industrial revolution, which was largely dependent upon steam power, a new form of energy. With the application of steam power to the cotton loom, England began her first cycle of prosperity. During this period, she put an end to Napoleon's troublemaking and achieved world leadership. The Napoleonic War was an important one, as world economic leadership hung in the balance. Napoleon's ambitions had to be dispensed with. After shipping him off to St. Helena, England found it in her best interests to pursue commerce peacefully and to engage in only minor foreign involvements that were not allowed to get out of hand. The earlier overexpansion of the cotton mills resulted in a terrible period of depression, a period that could be called England's creative destruction.

We call it a creative destruction because the prior excesses were eliminated so that the second great application of steam power—to the railroad—was able to attract the capital and labor necessary to germinate and bloom. In 1843, a 30-year golden age of prosperity began. Early in this second cycle, the Corn Laws were finally repealed. The age of cotton passed, and the age of the railroad commenced. The inflationary impact of the American Civil War provided the stimulus to heighten Britain's expectations. After these expectations were cooled, the overbuilding of the railroads began and the investment opportunities based on the further application of steam power were exhausted. By 1873, for the second time, Britain's economy was ready to crumble; however, *this time the situation was quite different from the bust of a half-century earlier* or from our 1929 crash, for that matter.

Now, a leadership class, the industrial leaders, who were committed to the ongoing prosperity, resolved not to let a period of bloodletting occur—at least not one like that experienced after the Napoleonic wars. They were unwilling to scrap everything and begin anew, so, rather than permit a creative destruction, they promoted a massive effort to patch up the system before the excesses were fully liquidated. The beast, depression, was tamed somewhat, without the widespread redistribution of capital assets that occurred during the prior depressionary period. Money from the big banks was channeled to the railroads, coal companies, and iron works, thus preventing the widespread bankruptcies and debt reduction which occurs during a creative destruction. The captains of industry felt more secure, since they were able to maintain control of the capital assets, and they were no longer willing to take the economic risks necessary to develop innovations. But, as the class structure solidified, it became harder for a new class of innovators and entrepreneurs to acquire the money and financing to develop the new ideas. As a consequence, the creative genius of the nation was lost and, increasingly, innovations were tried elsewhere.

Great Britain, as she entered her third cycle of prosperity (in 1897), felt the pressure of both the German and United States economies closing in on her. These new economies, which had already adopted England's methods and techniques, such as the development of the railroad, were in a position to exploit the innovative techniques (such as the automobile in America). As tensions increased, Germany called Britain's bluff as a world economic leader. Once again, there was sparring for economic world leadership. The result was World War I, and as Britain was unable to beat back the German challenge, the United States came to her aid. However, as world leadership hung in the balance, this war, unlike smaller wars, had to be won decisively. While Germany was ravaged, she was not yet ready to acquiesce in the United States' claim to world economic leadership. When she was able, Germany broke the Armistice and waged war—just as Napoleon had returned to wage his 100-day campaign. Again, the United States had to put an end to this persistent pretender. During these periods of war, Britain rather silently exited from center stage; the British phase of the industrial revolution ended, and the United States inherited the mantle of world leadership. The United States' first cycle of world economic leadership corresponds to Britain's third cycle.

Before a nation can assume economic leadership, four important factors are necessary. The first factor is the prior occurrence of an agricultural revolution; foods must not only be plentiful and cheap, but must become more efficiently produced so that both labor and capital are free to concentrate on industrial production. The second factor is an abundant and cheap source of labor, such as that provided by the huge migrations to the United States in the latter part of the nineteenth century. The third factor is the emergence of a new source of power or energy that can be economically exploited or transformed into an innovating industry, such as the steam power which led to the cotton mill and later the railroad. The fourth factor is a relatively large degree of political freedom from social restrictions or undue controls, so that a flexible social system or a risk-reward system can operate. This factor is usually achieved by internal political turmoil, or revolution, in which there is a realignment of political power or the freeing of a new social class, such as the rise of the bourgeoisie in England after their civil war in the late seventeenth century. In breaking up the old class constraints, a new group of people, who are more willing to take the economic risks, are provided with both the freedom and the motivation to exploit the new sources of economic growth.[4]

These conditions were present in England in the late eighteenth century and in the United States in the late nineteenth century. As a result of the social and economic mobility which followed the civil war in the seventeenth century, Britain was able to exploit steam power, a new form of energy. Then, with the dismantling of the Speenhamland system,[5] the rural population was dislodged from its traditional way of life and thrown into the labor force.

Though both Germany and America benefited from political realignment in the nineteenth century, the United States' innovating industry, the auto, was the outgrowth of a new source of energy, electric power (which was used to ignite the internal combustion engine), and therefore was able to support a wide range of further innovation. Germany's prosperity, on the other hand, was tied to the new chemical industry and not related to a new source of energy. Consequently, the United States, which was also the beneficiary of cheap and abundant agriculture and an influx of immigrants, was in a better position than Germany to assume world leadership.

The United States, after inheriting the railroad and a belief in free trade from England, was in a position to weather the worldwide depression of 1873–1897 rather well, and to begin her first cycle of world economic leadership. She was able to exploit the new energy source, which gave impetus to the development of the automobile. The United States emerged from World War I with heightened expectations, cooled these expectations, and then proceeded to over-build the automobile industry. The period of creative destruction was upon the United States.

Like England a hundred years earlier, the United States lacked

---

[4]Also, political stability is a necessary requisite.

[5]A form of poor relief whereby the rural poor were guaranteed a subsidy.

experience in such matters and was not prepared for the depression. Consequently, the excesses were rather fully liquidated. There was a relative redistribution of capital assets. That is, a lot of people lost their money, and people with good economic ideas could acquire assets.

Soon the United States emerged into its second cycle—its period of golden prosperity—when the industrial promises of the past 50 years were largely fulfilled. The age of the auto was replaced by the age of the computer, the second great application of electric power. The inflationary impact of the Vietnam war helped to heighten expectations in the United States. And these heightened expectations had to be cooled.

In the next depressionary period, we most likely will attempt to patch up the economy before the liquidation has run its course and the excesses of the past expansion are eliminated. The result should be a depressionary period more mild than the previous one: the levels of bankruptcies, unemployment, and debt reduction should fall short of those reached in the 1930s. Yet, in so doing, we will have fostered the conditions that will bring the end of our economic dominance—as in the case of Britain a hundred years ago. We will most likely be unwilling to take the economic and other risks necessary to develop and apply a new form of power. And, as the application of electric power will by then most likely have been pretty well exploited or its source of fuel nearly depleted, the economic innovations and strides are apt to occur elsewhere.

During the depressionary period, capital will probably be channeled into keeping the troubled businesses afloat, so that new entrepreneurs will probably not be able to get the capital necessary to develop a new energy source. The federal government is an unlikely candidate to meet this future challenge because political pressure makes it difficult for the government to pay the necessary short-term price. We have already seen how community after community has responded to the increased political power of middle-class people and banned the building of nuclear plants in their midst. They do not want to take the risk—in this case, the safety risk. Thus, during the third American cycle, economic mastery is likely to pass to a new nation. That is the cost of preventing a corrective liquidation.

The relationship between noneconomic events and economic

cycles, however, is not mystical or even predetermined. It results because depressions and long periods of prosperity, by serving as lessons of pain and pleasure, unleash important but unseen psychological forces that influence the way we think and act in our social and political sphere.

FOUR

MASS PSYCHOLOGY: THE KEY TO CYCLES

There are unseen psychological forces which both affect, and are affected by, the economy. Human behavior is different from what we have been taught. Human beings are not the objective creatures that we like to think; they are not economic individuals who act in their own rational self-interest. Rather, they are *psychological beings,* conditioned by their experiences, especially those experiences which serve as important lessons of pain or pleasure. When some lesson of pain—say, an economic depression—deflates their self-image, they perceive the world as risky. When some lesson of pleasure, such as a long period of prosperity, inflates their self-image, the world no longer appears so risky. These resulting perceptions of risk are the shared assumptions through which we see the world. By affecting our sense of power, *these assumptions color the way we think and act.* In one case, we attempt to avoid pain, while in another we seek to pursue pleasure, and in so doing, become receptive to those ideas, beliefs, and attitudes which rationalize our actions. Following an extended period of prosperity, the idea that we—men and women both—can be liberated from those economic chains which in the past have kept us from achieving personal fulfillment gets a ready response. Men and women adopt the psychology of affluence (and economic optimism) wherein they attempt to enjoy life, have fun, and become economic risk takers.

This mass psychology of optimism, once set off, takes on a life of its own. That is, it continues until people become excessively optimistic. As this psychology now helps influence economic events in its direction, other persons are induced to adopt these corresponding beliefs and expectations. As they rationalize that what has happened will continue to happen, they come to see less risk than actually exists. As a consequence, too many people become risk takers, a development which in turn creates the conditions for a big bust. This bust, or depression, then sets off a psychology of pessimism which continues until people become excessively pessimistic. They come to see more risk than really exists. This tendency leads to too many people becoming risk averters, a fact which, in turn, produces the conditions for a long expansion. In each case, this process usually occurs in three stages, as we can see by looking at the long economic cycle.

Our last expansionary phase began in 1949 against a background of excessive pessimism (Figure 2). The long period of economic pain that followed the 1929 collapse had humbled people. They came to see the world as a rather risky place and became skeptical of the economy's ability to provide prosperity. In such a world, the desire to become a risk taker was adversely affected. People cut their economic commitments to the bone and delayed their consumption so that they might build up savings. In short, most people became risk averters.

However, as the expansion of the 1950s rolled on, with nothing more than minor setbacks to interrupt it, a growing number of people came to recognize this emerging prosperity and began changing their behavior to coincide with it. They dipped into their savings in order to increase consumption, to buy stocks and real estate, and to become entrepreneurs; that is, they became risk takers. As the success of these new risk takers was recognized, others also increased their spending for both business and consumption purposes. The expansion was being fed.

Yet, the shared perception of a risky world acquired during the depression persisted and the vast majority of people remained risk averters. So, in the late 1950s, the rapid rise in the price of assets and cost of doing business left us unable to recruit new risk takers (owing to the high price of assets and cost of capital, other risk averters were discouraged from undertaking economic commitments). Hence, we could no longer generate the spending increases

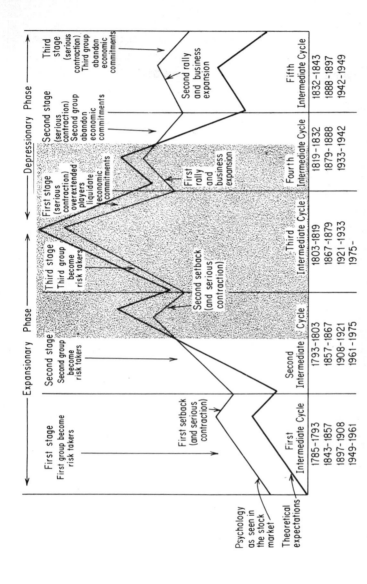

FIGURE 2 IDEAL LONG CYCLE. In about the middle of the second intermediate cycle, the psychological environment changes to optimism (shown by shaded area). At this time, profits are harder to come by and the performance of the economy becomes poorer. In about the middle of the fourth intermediate cycle, the psychological environment changes to pessimism. At this time, profits are easier to come by and the performance of the economy improves.

45

necessary to support the aggressive building of inventories and capital items that had taken place. The expansion had gotten ahead of itself and was now vulnerable to a serious setback. This ended the first stage of what we have called the *expansionary phase*.

As business profits fell and the stock market began slipping, some of the overextended risk takers were forced to liquidate. We got the contraction of 1960–1961, then the 1962 sharp break in the stock market, a more serious run of events than had occurred during the 1950s. The fears of 1929 were revived.

This period of more or less protracted expansion, followed by a contraction and stock market break more serious than those immediately preceding it, provides us with an intermediate cycle—that is, a smaller boom-bust period within the larger economic cycle.

Yet, now, in 1962, things were different. In providing a lesson of pleasure, the protracted and unexpected period of prosperity had begun to undermine our shared assumptions of a risky world. Many risk averters had been impressed by this run of prosperity, but were only willing to commit themselves to it provided they could do so on favorable terms: that is, the price of assets and the costs of doing business would have to show a big falloff. The contraction of 1960–1961 was providing such an opportunity. The willingness of these people to dip into their savings and increase their economic commitments cushioned this contraction and helped fuel another expansion. With this, *the first intermediate cycle was completed*. (See Figure 2.)

As the economy and stock market began to recover in 1962 without the experience of another 1929, more risk averters became convinced that this prosperity was "for real" and began to join in. The increased spending by this influx of new risk takers broadened the expansion and sent the stock market soaring to new all-time highs.

Suddenly, people began to notice that the economy was continuing to exceed their expectations. In an attempt to explain this phenomenon, the media and academia put the economy under their huge microscopes. They discovered that because of the government's commitment to maintain the level of demand, we could now expect more or less continued prosperity. The message was spread: We had entered a new economic age—one that was quite different from that of the thirties.

As the majority of people became optimistic that this prosperity would last, *the psychological environment changed.* The world no longer appeared to be so risky and, as a result, people became less concerned with avoiding pain and more interested in pursuing pleasure or participating in the good life. In order to justify—or rationalize—this change in their behavior, they readjusted their beliefs: they came to believe that they were entitled to enjoy life and grew impatient with the old societal constraints which they felt had in the past kept them from achieving personal fulfillment. In short, a vast psychological change occurred which led to a world that moved to a different beat, that was faster, louder, and more optimistic than in the 1930s.

In the economic sphere, the majority of people became risk takers—they became entrepreneurs, acquired stocks and real estate, or at the very least, cut into their savings so that they could increase their standard of living. Of course, these actions furthered the expansion even more, again pleasantly surprising people.

Yet, this new psychological environment soon had an important but unseen effect on the economy. One economist after the other—from Walter Heller to Milton Friedman—found that their economic models, which were based on the long psychological environment of 1938–1965 that had just come to an end, were no longer working.[1] In 1968, Dr. Arthur Burns, who was then chairman of the National Bureau of Economic Research, summed up the situation when he commented sadly, "The rules of economics are not working the same way they used to, the substantial sharp raises in wages . . . contrasts markedly with our experience in earlier recessions."

What had happened, of course, was that there had been a change in the way people were acting. This change soon began to undermine the very foundation upon which our long prosperity rested. Owing largely to an abundant amount of cheap or relatively cheap capital, labor, raw materials, fuel, and food, along with a relative shortage of industrial capacity—all of which had been the legacy of the prior depression—business profits for a long time had been

---

[1] Because the psychological background is constantly shifting, our economists are unable to find lasting causal relationships, or formulate absolute answers. Things work differently in each psychological environment.

rather easy to come by. This opportunity in turn had helped encourage the capital formation process. Now, however, with the advent of the new risk takers and the increased demand they generated, the cost of capital, labor, and raw materials skyrocketed; the long-term rate of interest surpassed the natural rate of interest. Because of these escalating costs and an increase in industrial capacity, this climate in which business profits were easy to acquire was ended, the capital formation process was impaired, and, by the early 1970s, pockets of weakness, such as Lockheed, the REITS,[2] and New York City, began showing up in the economy. The performance of the economy had become poorer, and we were again vulnerable to a serious contraction and stock market break. Thus ended the second stage of the expansionary phase.

As business activity slowed and the stock market started down, some of the overextended risk takers, who now were more numerous than in 1961–1962, were forced to liquidate. We got another serious contraction, that of 1973–1975, along with a severe break in the stock market. Once again the fear that we were headed for a depression surfaced.

Although the economy was not as healthy as it had been in the 1950s, there were still many strong areas. And they could bolster the weak so that our problems could be patched up. Money was channeled (through the banking system) from the many profitable areas of the economy to Italy, New York City, Lockheed, and many of the less-developed countries (to help offset their increased costs of energy) so that these weak sisters would not go under and drag the world economy down with them. Also, the government cut taxes so that aggregate demand would be increased. As a result, corporate profitability was restored at least temporarily, and we emerged from this serious contraction to begin another expansion. *The second intermediate cycle was now completed.*

We were at the point in this cycle comparable with 1921 in the last cycle. In the 1920s, when the economy began expanding again, those risk averters whose earlier experience (provided by the depressionary period of 1873–1897) had been more painful than had that of the others joined in. Though they had not participated during the

---

[2] Real Estate Investment Trusts.

second stage, these risk averters had become aware of the fact they were now in the minority. Most other people had views different from theirs, and this disparity, of course, was likely to make them more uncomfortable with their convictions. So, as the economy began another sustained economic advance, its third, and as these people saw that in the pursuit of the good life, they were being left behind, they could no longer resist conforming to the lesson of pleasure. They became believers in the prosperity and, with their conversion, started dipping into their savings to expand the level of their spending. This spending helped fuel the third stage in this expansionary phase.

By 1929 we had experienced three stages in the expansionary phase and, as almost everyone had come to believe in the prosperity, the psychological environment had become overdone; that is, too many people now wanted to become risk takers. The excessive pessimism which characterized the 1890s had been replaced with an excessive optimism.

The economy was now ready for a huge bust. And the government could not prevent this collapse by cutting taxes and thus attempt to infuse an injection of liquidity into the economy. What had happened during the third stage was that as more and more people had come to believe—and rationalized this belief by arguing that "another depression could not possibly occur"—the economy began to appear less risky. Our memory of a real depression was dimmed and there was a lack of appreciation of the real risk that does exist. Expectations became way too high in relation to our economy.

Such an atmosphere results in a less cautious attitude among businesspeople; the less qualified ones become entrepreneurs, less promising investment opportunities are pursued as the more promising investment ideas become exhausted, and workers become less concerned about their jobs. We enter an atmosphere where business miscalculations increase, where overborrowing and overspending become prevalent, and where many people are willing to pay ever increasing prices to acquire stocks, real estate, or raw materials (that is, until they are no longer able to). And any new stimulus only enforces this same economic behavior; people increase their borrowing, bankers make more unsound loans, producers attempt to raise their prices even more, and so on—until something gives. Perhaps the price of energy rises too high, or maybe the number of unsound loans becomes enormous: some problem finally becomes unmanageable and sets off a liquidation which shatters an overdone psychology.

One would think that this imbalance in the economy should be perceived. However, people believe in this prosperity and people who believe usually do not listen to arguments contrary to their belief, no matter how logical. Throughout the 1920s, many doomsayers had cried "wolf" and "wolf" had never come. We had survived the Florida building collapse in the mid–1920s, and time and again the Fed had warned of inflation, and inflation had failed to bring on hard times.

Again, in the 1970s, we have heard persuasive arguments that due to the high cost of energy, or the huge level of loans to the underdeveloped countries, or the exhaustion of our resources foreseen by the prestigious Club of Rome, our prosperity cannot endure. Yet, people's experience has been one of continual economic expansion. These problems of the seventies have been around at least since the serious contraction of 1973–1974, and the economy, though shaken, has *not* turned down into a depression. Gradually, people come to see that the worst usually does not happen and do not buy the scare talk. When confronted by the doomsayers, the mass of people resort to faith, not logic, for, in this respect, faith seems the better guide. And, to change a belief which rests largely on faith, people must experience the opposite.

There is no way out short of a collapse. Behavior must be altered so that our excessive economic commitments are reduced, costs are lowered, liquidity is rebuilt, and expectations are reduced. Such a change requires a lesson of pain—that is, a depression.

The depressionary phase of the cycle also occurred in three stages (see Figure 2). In the first stage, the depression of 1929–1933 shattered an overdone psychological environment, one in which people had been excessively optimistic.[3] During the subsequent recovery in the economy, a lot of people who had been affected by the wrench-

---

[3] This completed the third intermediate cycle; during the depressionary phase, we got two more intermediate cycles.

ing lesson of pain eased out of their economic commitments or at least refrained from increasing their spending. As a result, we got another economic contraction of major proportions in 1937, which was the beginning of the second stage down. During this stage, the majority of people became disillusioned and lost faith in the economy. The psychological environment changed to one where people now wanted to be risk averters, and this about-face soon led to a real improvement in the performance of the economy.

However, because the new psychology of pessimism affected people's willingness to spend, we got yet another serious contraction, that of 1945–1946. This was the third stage down, and during it people became excessively pessimistic. As too many people became risk averters and took precautions against renewed depression, an immunity to such further depression was built into the economy. We got a substantial fall in business costs, a reduction in productive capacity, the buildup of a hoard of liquidity, and a backlog of promising investment opportunities. These conditions laid the foundation for another long period of expansion.

These periods of depression play an important part in our world. They are not a malfunction of a capitalistic economy but, rather, a necessary lesson of pain which, by changing behavior, allows the economy to regenerate itself. What happens is that during good times, our beliefs and expectations become overdone. That is, they become too much for the event that spawned them. People must be jolted back to reality once again. It takes an alternate lesson to do this: a lesson of pain if man has been responding to pleasure. Neither the Keynesians nor the monetarists understand that we cannot alter behavior without causing some accompanying lesson of pain.

Perhaps a certain amount of human suffering may be the price that must be paid for social and economic progress. For, if new ways of doing things are to emerge, power—at least over capital assets—must be passed from one group to another. Unfortunately, this is not likely to happen without chaos and conflict. Had our ancestors been able to avoid conflict and remain in a state of harmony, the economic prosperity upon which our contemporary civilization is based would not exist and we would not be "we."

Because human psychology is slow to change, a broad economic move usually occurs in three stages.[4] The first stage begins when some unexpected event shatters an overdone psychological environment. Yet, while some people respond immediately to this new lesson, most people, as they find it outside their past experience, do not believe it. They need more evidence—that is, a second stage. Typically, the majority become convinced during the second stage and therefore the psychological background changes. People begin to act differently, and their behavior soon affects the performance of the economy.

However, people are reluctant to believe that the economy has changed and they resist conforming to this change. For example, most people do not begin abandoning their economic commitments during a contraction following the second stage of an expansionary phase. As a result, we get a third stage up, during which the die-hards join in. The psychological environment becomes overdone, and the resulting economic behavior provides a fertile breeding ground for some contrary economic event which, by shattering this overdone psychology, becomes an important and extended economic move. As we shall see, the important moves in the economy, the stock market, and stocks and commodities are preceded by excessive optimism or excessive pessimism.

What happens is that people catch on to the meaning of their important experiences and bring their beliefs and expectations into line with such experiences. However, as the majority of people recognize their experiences, these same beliefs and expectations are pushed too far—or become overdone. Thus, this same catching-on process has resulted in a paradox. When too many people catch on to their external world (economic events), they create the conditions to change it.

---

[4] A country's period of economic leadership also seems to encompass three stages, with each long economic cycle being one stage. Leadership is lost during the country's third stage, and during this same cycle another country is beginning its first stage. England ended her period of leadership during the 1897–1949 cycle, which was also the first stage of the United States leadership. In this case of economic leadership, there is an increase in the number of people participating in the economy: That is, there is a buildup in the middle and working classes who, unlike the poor, have savings or incomes above a sustenance level and so can increase the level of their economic commitments if they choose to do so.

People, or at least the majority of people, it seems, are victims of their experience. They see things in light of what has happened in the past and commit themselves to (i.e., respond to) one phase of a cycle. Like most politicians and generals, they find themselves continually fighting the last war. So, perhaps we learn the lessons, or at least some of the lessons, of history too well.

Let us now turn our attention to the intermediate cycle.

FIVE

INTERMEDIATE CYCLES

During each long economic cycle there appear to be five intermediate cycles. (A three-staged expansionary phase followed by a three-staged depressionary phase has occurred during each long cycle, giving us five intermediate cycles.[1]) An intermediate cycle consists of a period of sustained economic growth—that is, a series of traditional business expansions (the two- to four-year variety) broken by only mild recessions—followed by a serious contraction. These serious contractions, unlike the milder ones, are accompanied by a severe falloff in industrial activity, a sharp break in the stock market, and an extended decline in long-term interest rates. The severity of these contractions leads businesspeople, consumers, and investors to become more cautious and attempt to reduce their economic commitments and increase their liquidity—that is, their cash on hand. Business managers reduce inventories, eliminate debt, and lay off workers. Consumers cut down on their purchases and build up their savings. And investors cut back on their holdings and purchases of stocks. As a result, the cost of capital and labor[2]

---

[1]There are five such cycles because both the third stage of the expansionary phase and the first stage of the depressionary phase occur during the third intermediate cycle (see Figure 2).

[2]Since World War II and the advent of big unions, wages have continued to increase, though at a lesser rate, during these serious contractions. However, much of this increase is offset by the gain in productivity that takes place at this time. As a consequence, the cost of labor, rather than coming down, levels off.

comes down, thus enhancing corporate profitability which, in turn, leads to another period of sustained economic growth. Thus, a serious contraction, unlike a milder one which does not induce a more cautious attitude, provides the foundation for the next intermediate cycle.

We can see how this works by doing an anatomy of the intermediate cycle which began in 1921 and lasted until 1933 (Chart 4). This intermediate cycle followed the contraction of 1920–1921, the most severe of any since the prior depression. Industrial production fell 30% and the stock market broke 47%, its worst break in 35 years. Confidence was shaken and a great deal of pessimism was created. Businesspeople eliminated debt, cut wages, and instituted other broad cost-cutting measures, while consumers began to increase their savings. As a result, a great deal of liquidity was acquired. Also, the cost of capital and labor was reduced, laying the basis for increased corporate profitability.

By mid-1921 the liquidation of business inventories had gone too far. The promising investment opportunities which had not been undertaken at the end of the prior intermediate cycle, because of the prohibitive costs of capital and labor, could now be developed. As business owners began to replenish their inventories, the first business expansion of the intermediate cycle began and was accompanied by a rise in stock prices. Yet, the recent unhappy experience of 1920–1921 had left a cautious attitude on the part of businesspeople, consumers, and investors. Business spending for capital items increased only moderately. Consumers loosened their purse strings only gradually. And in the stock market, investors stressed the conservative dividend payers. Thus, this expansion did not develop the boomlike conditions and speculative excesses seen in the previous expansion of 1919. In fact, long-term interest rates continued to fall throughout the early part of this business expansion. Usually this drop occurs only during the first expansion of an intermediate cycle and is a sign that business and consumer demands are not increasing too rapidly—or are not eating up the reservoir of liquidity that has been recently acquired.

By 1923, the expansion began to quicken and, as business managers further increased the level of their inventories, there was a sharp rise in commodity prices. The Federal Reserve Board, deter-

Intermediate Cycle of 1921-1933

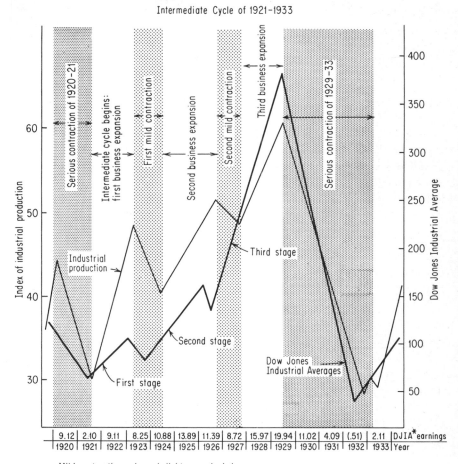

Mild contractions shown in light gray shaded area.
Serious contractions shown in dark gray shaded area.

*From 1920 untill 1928 is estimated from Commercial and Financial Chronicle 7/11/46.

CHART 4

mined not to let this expansion get out of hand as the previous one
had, increased the discount rate. A higher discount rate leads member banks to borrow less from the Fed and, in turn, to reduce their
loans to the business community. As the supply of credit was
reduced, long-term interest rates rose. Business executives and
investors began to fear that these increased costs—for both capital

and raw materials—would put a strain on business earnings. With the debacle of 1920–1921 still fresh in their minds, they quickly cut their spending, and this reduction helped lead us into a mild recession. Industrial production fell only 15% during 1923-1924 and the Dow Jones Industrial Average declined 18%, ending the first stage of the long bull market in stocks. This recession was mild because businesspeople had not exhausted their buying power during the 1921–1923 expansion; they were still quite liquid and were able to take advantage of a moderate falloff in the cost of capital and labor to increase their spending for capital items. This spending fueled the next economic advance, restored business profits, and led to the second stage in the stock market's long rise to 1929.

As the second business expansion commenced—in mid-1924—the pace of economic activity quickened. The mildness of the recent recession, together with a resurgence of business earnings, led to a more adventuresome attitude on the part of consumers, investors, and businesspeople. Consumers dipped into their savings and began to increase their spending. The stock market surpassed its old high of 119, set in 1919,[3] and began attracting an expanding amount of public participation. Business managers became bolder, increasing inventories, taking on debt, and hiring more workers. New businesses appeared on the scene. This increased competition led to additional industrial capacity which, in turn, made it more difficult for business to raise prices. And, as business costs were also rising, reflecting the increased demand for capital and labor, profit margins came under serious pressure for the first time since this intermediate cycle began. Business profits experienced a big decline, and the aggregate earnings of the stocks composing the Dow Jones Industrial Averages fell to their lowest level in four years. This decrease led to the second recession of this intermediate cycle. And stock prices broke 16%, ending the second stage of this long bull market. Fears of 1920–1921 were revived again and the banking authorities, who at that time were held responsible for prosperity, began aggressively to stimulate the economy. The Fed cut the discount rate during 1926, and then again in 1927, ensuring an increased supply of credit. This

-----

[3]Dow Jones Industrial Averages.

additional monetary stimulus boosted purchasing power so that businesses could raise their prices and restore corporate profitability. As the increased competition had only just begun, and as consumers, businessowners, and investors had not yet exhausted their liquidity, this recession was also quite mild. Industrial production fell only 6%. Soon, another business expansion began.

As we began the third business expansion in late 1927, people became even bolder. The experience of two rather mild recessions, which were unable to stop the tide of rising profits, led people finally to forget the serious contraction of 1920–1921 and lose their caution. The stock market made new highs again and the third stage of this bull market was swept along by a mounting speculative enthusiasm. The public's appetite for common stocks was whetted by six years of rising earnings, along with the gaining popularity of Edgar Laurence Smith's book *Common Stocks as Long-Term Investments*, published in 1924, which showed that common stocks had significantly outperformed bonds during almost any period of the last 50 years. The monetary stimulus of 1926–1927, combined with the remainder of the liquidity that had been hoarded since 1921, provided the public with the ammunition to participate in this bull market. The volume of trading expanded far beyond anything seen in the past. With the rallying cry that "a stock with good long-term prospects is always a good investment," the public, which had shied away from stocks when they were cheap, was now willing to pay almost any price to "join in." The Dow Jones Industrial Average hit 381 in September of 1929—a rise in excess of 500% from its low of 63 in 1921. And the last 190 points of this rise occurred after February 1928. This rise in the stock market reflected not only the increase in business profits which had occurred during the intermediate cycle, but also, as confidence in the economy grew, an increased willingness to pay more for a given dollar of earnings. In the parlance of Wall Street, price-earnings ratios expanded.

This excessive optimism was by no means confined to Wall Street. A spreading euphoria clouded the judgment of business managers, bankers, and workers alike. Business owners increased the level of their spending dramatically, raised prices indiscriminately, and became less concerned about costs. The growing army of risk takers exhausted the profitable investment opportunities and began imitating the successful business enterprises. More and more new automobile companies sprang up, as did more companies to supply these new auto companies, and the eventual result was a great deal of excess capacity. Not only did the level of debt formation increase, but as the bankers financed the less profitable investment opportunities, the quality of their loans deteriorated. Simultaneously, workers, feeling less need to worry about their jobs, were putting less effort into their work. The resulting rapid rise in business costs surpassed the ability of business managers to raise prices, and this once again put a strain on profit margins.

In 1929, the Fed publicized its concern with the soundness of the expansion and raised the discount rate sharply. Yet, scarcely anyone noticed. Just as the contraction of 1920–1921 had generated a great deal of pessimism, the eight years of increasing prosperity, higher earnings, and rising stock prices had made everyone overly optimistic. People had come to believe in this prosperity. The economists (whom we like to think should have known better) were no exception. They, too, fell victim to this excessive optimism. As the performance of the economy continued to exceed their forecasts, they began to think we were onto something new. This something new was that following the serious contraction of 1920–1921, the Fed had discovered its errors and was now able to provide a steady hand on the economy by maintaining credit stability. As prosperity was now easier to achieve, or so we all thought, we no longer needed to worry about serious contractions. Any resulting decline in both business activity and stock prices, due to a policy of mild credit restraint by the Fed, would, as in the past, be only temporary before the upward march was resumed. Thus, businesspeople were not worried and in the stock market no one, or almost no one, sold.

In mid-1929, a contraction began when business spending fell in response to the declining investment opportunities. But this time, conditions were different from those preceding the previous two recessions. The hoard of liquidity had finally been spent, so there was no longer a latent demand for goods and services to help check the contraction. Moreover, as the market for goods had become saturated, monetary stimulus would no longer allow business managers to raise prices. Now, when business profits fell, some of the excessive economic commitments had to be liquidated, and this step fueled the contraction so that it became serious.

In a period of 10 weeks during the fall of 1929, the Dow Jones Industrial Average lost nearly 60% of its entire 8-year advance, wiping out the capital of an estimated 1 million people who owned stocks on margin. This sharp fall in the value of people's assets adversely affected both consumer and business confidence. As business earnings fell, workers were fired, inventories were cut to the bone, and capital spending dried up, leading to the most severe contraction in our history. Industrial production fell 50%, unemployment reached 25% of the labor force, business and bank failures became widespread, confidence was shattered, and the Dow Jones Industrial Average continued to fall until it reached 41 in July of 1932. During this decline, the 1921 low of 63 was taken out. (This was a significant event. Within a few months after the low was broken, the DJIA bottomed out and never reached such a low level again.) People became pessimistic and shied away from economic commitments. The Republicans were held responsible for this debacle and were voted out of office.

Yet, by 1933, a lot of the imbalances had been worked off. Marginal enterprises were eliminated. Excess capacity was reduced, debt was cut back, and business costs were sharply lower, since long-term interest rates had fallen and workers were now eager for a chance to work hard. We were ready to begin another intermediate cycle, although this one would be a different type because the liquidation in the economy had not fully run its course.

In summary, then, the intermediate cycle of 1921–1933 contained three traditional business expansions separated by two relatively mild recessions. The economic advance corresponded to a long three-stage bull market in stocks that reached its high during the third business expansion of this intermediate cycle. (Note that each stage was punctuated by a 15% decline in the DJIA.) This economic and stock market advance was similar in character to the advances that preceded and followed it.

There were four other intermediate cycles that occurred during the expansionary phase of the last two long cycles, and each of these was quite similar to the one just described (see Chart 5).

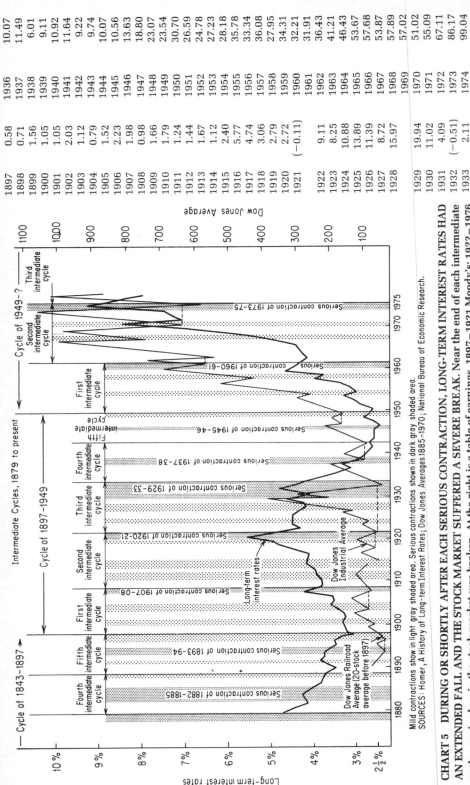

Year	Earnings	Year	Earnings
1897	0.58	1936	10.07
1898	0.71	1937	11.49
1899	1.56	1938	6.01
1900	1.05	1939	9.11
1901	1.05	1940	10.92
1902	2.03	1941	11.64
1903	1.12	1942	9.22
1904	0.79	1943	9.74
1905	1.52	1944	10.07
1906	2.23	1945	10.56
1907	1.98	1946	13.63
1908	0.98	1947	18.80
1909	1.66	1948	23.07
1910	1.79	1949	23.54
1911	1.24	1950	30.70
1912	1.44	1951	26.59
1913	1.67	1952	24.78
1914	1.12	1953	27.23
1915	2.40	1954	28.18
1916	5.77	1955	35.78
1917	4.74	1956	33.34
1918	3.06	1957	36.08
1919	2.79	1958	27.95
1920	2.72	1959	34.31
1921	(−0.11)	1960	32.21
		1961	31.91
1922	9.11	1962	36.43
1923	8.25	1963	41.21
1924	10.88	1964	46.43
1925	13.89	1965	53.67
1926	11.39	1966	57.68
1927	8.72	1967	53.87
1928	15.97	1968	57.89
		1969	57.02
1929	19.94	1970	51.02
1930	11.02	1971	55.09
1931	4.09	1972	67.11
1932	(−0.51)	1973	86.17
1933	2.11	1974	99.04
1934	3.91	1975	75.66
1935	6.34	1976	96.72

Mild contractions show in light gray shaded area. Serious contractions shown in dark gray shaded area.

SOURCES: Homer, A History of Long-term Interest Rates; Dow Jones Averages 1885–1970; National Bureau of Economic Research.

CHART 5   DURING OR SHORTLY AFTER EACH SERIOUS CONTRACTION, LONG-TERM INTEREST RATES HAD AN EXTENDED FALL AND THE STOCK MARKET SUFFERED A SEVERE BREAK. Near the end of each intermediate cycle, a prior low in the stock market was broken. At the right is a table of earnings. 1897–1921 Moody's; 1922–1976 DJIA; from 1922–1928 estimated in Commercial and Financial Chronicle 7/11/46.

THE EXPANSIONARY PHASE OF THE 1897–1949 CYCLE

First intermediate cycle	1897–1908
Second intermediate cycle	1908–1921
Third intermediate cycle	1921–1933

THE EXPANSIONARY PHASE OF THE PRESENT CYCLE

First intermediate cycle	1949–1961
Second intermediate cycle	1961–1975

Each of these intermediate cycles lasted approximately 12 years. The first recession was usually surprisingly mild. The falloff in industrial activity, stock prices, and interest rates was well below that of the serious contraction during the previous intermediate cycle (see Table 5-1). During the second recession, the leaders—either the banking system in earlier days or more recently the government— came to the aid of the economy and applied a massive dose of stimulation (such as decreases in the discount rate in 1914 and 1926, and more recently, in 1958 and 1970, massive budget deficits). This operation was a success, in that the recession proved to be relatively mild, and we soon got renewed strength in industrial production, consumer buying, and stock prices.

Typically, by the third traditional business expansion of the intermediate cycle, the pessimism which was so apparent at the beginning of the cycle turns to excessive optimism as people have come to believe in this prosperity.[4] Investors are paying exceedingly high premiums to own stocks, and business managers are also acting recklessly, increasing inventories, capital expenditures, and debt beyond what would seem sensible, and becoming careless about costs. As a consequence, vigorous economic growth can no longer take place.

In order to stop this indiscriminate building of economic commitments and allow another period of economic growth to occur, it is

---

[4]A three-stage upswing similar to that during the expansionary phase of the larger cycle has occurred. However, in this case, it is primarily the psychology of one group of investors, such as those who are quick to respond to new lessons and who therefore had become risk takers during the first stage of the larger cycle, which swings from pessimism to excessive optimism in three stages. It is the liquidation by some of the overextended members of this group that fuels the subsequent serious contraction.

TABLE 5-1 FIVE INTERMEDIATE CYCLES OF THE EXPANSIONARY PHASE

Era of:	Beginning date	Duration in months	Dow Jones corresponding stage in stock market	Peak[a] earnings (in dollars)	Rise in interest rates during first 16 months (percent)
1897–1949 cycle					
1897–1908					
1st expansion	June 1897	24	41–87[d]	1.56	1
2nd expansion	Dec. 1900	21	72–129[d]	2.03	2½
3rd expansion	Aug. 1904	33	88–138[d]	2.23	1½
	Total rise in DJIA from low to high: 235%				
1908–1921					
1st expansion	June 1908	19	36–88	1.79	1
2nd expansion	Jan. 1912	12	—	1.67	5
3rd expansion	Dec. 1914	45	54–110	5.77	6
4th expansion	March 1919	10	65–119	—	21
	Total rise in DJIA from low to high: 425%				
1921–1933					
1st expansion	July 1921	22	63–105	9.11	3
2nd expansion	July 1924	27	85–162	13.89	2
3rd expansion	Nov. 1927	21	135–381	19.94	10
	Total rise in DJIA from low to high: 500%				
1949–? cycle					
1949–1961					
1st expansion	Oct. 1949	45	161–521	30.70	4
2nd expansion	Aug. 1954	35	"	36.08	9
3rd expansion	April 1958	25	419–685 566–734[g]	34.31	25
	Total rise in DJIA from low to high: 350%				
1961–1975					
1st expansion	Feb. 1961	71	535–995	57.68	6
2nd expansion	April 1967	31	744–985	57.89	25
3rd expansion	Nov. 1970	36	631–1051	99.04	8
	Total rise in DJIA from low to high: 97%				
1975–?					
1st expansion	March 1975		577–?		3

[a]1897–1921, Moody's stock indexes, 1921–1975, Dow Jones Industrial Averages.

[b]Before 1919, AT&T index.

[c]Severity is obtained by taking an average of the financial magnitude of the fall, and the fall in industrial production; the financial magnitude is derived by adding the percentage fall in interest rates to the length of the fall (months) and then averaging this figure with the fall in stock prices.

Beginning date of contraction	Falloff in industrial production[b] (percent)	Fall in stock market (percent)	Fall in long-term interest rates		Severity[c]
			(percent)	(months)	
1st contraction: June 1899	10	17	3	15	14
2nd contraction: Sept. 1902	17	31	3	18	21
3rd contraction: May 1907	47	42	10	15	30
1st contraction: Jan. 1910	8	28	1	6	13
2nd contraction: Jan. 1913	18	23	4	16	20
3rd contraction: Sept. 1918	19	40	8	2	22
4th contraction: Jan. 1920	30	47	23	28	39
1st contraction: May 1923	15	18	7	27	20
2nd contraction: Oct. 1926	6	16	7	16	13
3rd contraction: August 1929	50	89	39	54	71
1st contraction: July 1953	9	13	15	9	14
2nd contraction: July 1957	12	19	15	18	19
3rd contraction: May 1960	7	27[e]	10	40	23
1st contraction: Dec. 1966	3	25	8	5	11
2nd contraction: Nov. 1969	8	36	16	8	19
3rd contraction: Nov. 1973	15	45	15[f]	35	29

[a]The Dow Jones Railroad Average was used, as at this time the rails were the blue chips.

[e]Total decline; a smaller fall of 17% occurred from 1959 to 1960.

[f]So far.

[g]Beginning of next intermediate cycle.

necessary to generate enough pessimism so that business planners become cautious and eliminate some of the waste and misjudgments that have arisen during the past period of sustained economic growth. To create this attitude, another serious contraction is required.

In the intermediate cycle of 1908–1921, this excessive optimism did not occur during the third business expansion. In that case, the second business expansion was unusually short—one of only two expansions in our economic history that lasted less than 18 months—so that there was not sufficient time to generate much optimism. Aggregate earnings as seen in Moody's stock index did not surpass the level achieved during the prior expansion (Table 5-1). In this case, it was during the third business expansion that a buildup of optimism occurred, and it was not until the fourth expansion that this optimism became excessive. At that time, we got a great deal of speculative activity, a surging inflation, and a sharp rise in long-term interest rates.

Following the third business expansion of these intermediate cycles (the fourth expansion in the 1908–1921 cycle), we got a serious contraction. The falloff in industrial production and stock prices was much more severe than in the two previous recessions. The break in the stock market was the worst in at least 25 years and the low made during the last recession was broken during this time. This is a sign that confidence is shaken and people are becoming pessimistic. And as people shy away from economic commitments and begin increasing their liquidity, long-term interest rates have an extended fall, which, in the past, lasted at least 15 months.[5] This lays the foundation for another period of economic growth.[6]

Of course, these intermediate cycles are not identical. There were three intermediate cycles in each expansionary phase, as listed earlier. In the first two of these intermediate cycles, the serious

---

[5]They also broke at least 10%.

[6]In the 1960–1961 contraction, the falloff in industrial activity was not so severe as during the prior two recessions. However, it was this recession which shook confidence, stopped the rise in long-term interest rates, and led to a severe break in the stock market.

contraction did not degenerate into a depression, as the longer term expansionary phase was still healthy.[7] And the break in the stock market did not continue until the low made at the beginning of the intermediate cycle was taken out, as in 1921–1933—it lasted only until the low made during the preceding recession was taken out. Confidence was merely shaken—not lost as it was later, after the third intermediate cycle.

During the 1949–1961 intermediate cycle, unlike the other intermediate cycles, the bull market in stocks had only two stages (see Chart 5). The first stage in this bull market spanned the first two business expansions. This was so because the break accompanying the first recession was *less* than 15%. In the past, it has taken a break of 15% or more to indicate that there has been a significant interruption in the psychology fueling the advance so that a stage of the bull market was completed. As a result of this extended first stage, the second stage accompanied the third business expansion of the intermediate cycle.

The third stage of this bull market occurred in the beginning of the next intermediate cycle in the economy: that is, following the serious contraction of 1960–1961, the stock market recovered from its moderate break (more than 15%) without having broken a prior low, and began another advance. However, as a result, the intermediate cycle of 1961–1975 began before a sufficient amount of pessimism had been generated. As a consequence, the rate of economic growth was slowed. If we were to get vigorous growth in the economy, it was necessary to complete the liquidation of excesses that had occurred during the prior intermediate cycle. And this occurred when, following President Kennedy's rollback of the price increase in steel in 1962, the business and financial community, thinking that we had entered a new business climate in which business profits would be hard to come by, panicked. The liquidation, occurring chiefly but not completely in the stock market, was resumed. The stock market broke over 25%, its worst break since 1938, and took

---

[7]These serious contractions do not extend until a level of excessive pessimism is achieved, as long as there are still other groups who have not yet joined in waiting on the sidelines.

out the low made in 1960—the break accompanying the last recession. Enough people had become pessimistic so that the conditions for a period of sustained economic expansion were now there.

Also, in the 1961–1975 intermediate cycle, in contrast with that of 1921–1933, speculative activity in both the stock market and the economy appeared early, that is, during the second business expansion and the second stage of the bull market. This activity developed in part because the previous intermediate cycle had ended with less of a bang than any of the other intermediate cycles. The recession of 1960–1961 was not so severe and the stock market break, though the largest in 25 years, was quite a bit less than the 40% breaks accompanying the other severe contractions. Consequently, in this intermediate cycle, not as in the other intermediate cycles, the stock market exceeded its old high during the first business expansion. (This rise usually happens during the second business expansion.) This was a sign that optimism was returning sooner than normal. Also, unlike its response in other intermediate cycles, the government applied a great deal of stimulus (which led to the 1968 deficit in the federal budget—the largest deficit since World War II) during (rather than after) the second expansion of the intermediate cycle. This action led to a surge of speculative activity in the stock market unlike anything seen since 1929. And, as in the 1920s, a study was made. Published in 1964 by Professors James Lorie and Lawrence Fischer of the University of Chicago, it showed that the rate of return in the stock market from 1926–1960 was 9% per annum compounded—far greater than most alternative mediums. By 1967, the public was snapping up new issues and pushing glamour stocks to unheard-of heights. Institutional investors were abandoning their traditional long-term goals and, instead, were emphasizing yearly, and then even quarterly, performance. The resulting increase in volume was so huge that the back offices of brokerage firms could not keep up with the necessary paperwork.[8] As this same psychology was occurring in the business community, the economy was also showing signs of becoming overextended at this time.

However, owing to the pumping of excessive amounts of money

---

[8]The last time that had happened was in 1929, another time of excessive speculative activity.

into the economy via even larger budget deficits, the following recession (1969–1970) was not severe, and a pickup in business activity soon began. While the third business expansion (1970–1973) was accompanied by a gigantic inflation, the stock market did not experience a great deal of speculative activity at this time, and thus led many to believe that the market was basically healthy. Yet, as a speculative binge had already occurred in this intermediate cycle, there was no need for it to appear again. And, following this third business expansion, we experienced the severe contraction of 1973–1974.

During the depressionary phase of the long cycle, these intermediate cycles do not behave the same way. The economic growth which occurs at the beginning of the intermediate cycle cannot be sustained. The explanation is that we have a different overriding psychology, set off by the loss of confidence in our economy, which induces people to reduce, rather than increase, their economic commitments. After one vigorous business expansion which is accompanied by a single-stage rise in the stock market, industrial production usually falls severely, the stock market experiences a sharp break, and confidence is shattered again. This contraction, which follows the first expansion of the intermediate cycle, is a serious one. Yet, unlike those which occur during the expansionary phase, these serious contractions do not set off a new period of sustained economic expansion. The renewal of real economic expansion, wherein we have a strong rise in capital spending as well as in stock prices, is delayed until after we have experienced another contraction, which is fueled by the continuing reduction of economic commitments. During this second contraction of the intermediate cycle, the Dow Jones Industrial Average usually breaks the low made during the serious contraction, signifying that pessimism in both the stock market and the business community has become excessive.[9] When pessimism becomes excessive, the *cut* in inventories, capital spend-

---

[9]These downswings appear to contain two stages rather than the typical three. This may be because following a vicious downswing such as occurred in 1929–1933, people's convictions are shaken. As a result, during the first stage of each new downswing, most of the members of a new group become pessimistic, and in the second stage of the downswing, they become excessively pessimistic.

ing, and debt is overdone, just as the *buildup* of these items was overdone when optimism was excessive. We can then begin a new intermediate cycle as the need to rebuild our economic stock of goods allows a subsequent expansion to pick up momentum and generate a full head of steam.

There have been two intermediate cycles during the depressionary phase of each long cycle. Consequently, since 1879, the depressionary phase prior to the last long cycle, there have been four such intermediate cycles.

THE DEPRESSIONARY PHASE OF THE 1843–1897 CYCLE
First intermediate cycle   1879–1888
Second intermediate cycle   1888–1897

THE DEPRESSIONARY PHASE OF THE 1897–1949 CYCLE
First intermediate cycle   1933–1942
Second intermediate cycle   1942–1949

These four intermediate cycles were quite similar (see Table 5-2). A serious contraction usually followed the first extended business

TABLE 5-2   TWO INTERMEDIATE CYCLES OF THE DEPRESSIONARY PHASE

Era of:	Beginning date	Duration in months	Corresponding stage in stock market*		Peak earnings
1933–1942					
First expansion	March 1933	50	41–194	375% rise	11.49
Second expansion	June 1938	46†	98–158	60% rise	11.64
1942–1949					
First expansion	April 1942‡	34§	92–212	125% rise	13.63
Second expansion	October 1945	37	163–193	19% rise	23.07

*Dow Jones Industrial Averages.

†Until April 1942, when prior low in stock market was taken out.

‡When intermediate cycle began.

§From April 1942.

¶However, stock prices experience a big decline.

expansion of the intermediate cycle.[10] Both industrial production and stock prices fell more sharply than they would during the following contraction. And long-term interest rates continued their decline, making new lows. This serious contraction cast a pall over both business and the stock market for the remainder of the intermediate cycle. Businesspeople were reluctant to extend their economic commitments. As a result, the following expansion was rather moderate, not being accompanied by a major upturn in capital spending, and it was followed by yet another wave of liquidation. During this second contraction of the intermediate cycle, the Dow Jones Industrial Average usually broke the low made during the serious contraction. This was a sign that a sufficient amount of pessimism had been generated in both the stock market and the business community, so that a new intermediate cycle could begin. Even in the intermediate cycle of 1933–1942, when the economy did not experience a second contraction, this liquidation in the stock market (wherein the DJIA took out its prior low), following the outbreak of World War II,

------

[10]When this expansion was short, as in the intermediate cycle beginning in 1888, the serious contraction came after the second business expansion of the intermediate cycle. In that case, the first expansion had lasted only 27 months, well below that of the first expansions in the other intermediate cycles.

	Beginning date	Falloff in industrial production (percent)	Fall in stock prices (percent)	Fall in long-term interest rates		
				(percent)	(months)	Severity
First contraction	May 1937	31	49	23	55	47
No contraction¶			42			
First contraction	February 1945	30	23	8	17	27
Second contraction	November 1948	8	16	10	17	15

during a modest expansion generated a sufficient amount of pessimism so that the expansion was able to pick up a full head of steam.

To summarize: there are five serious contractions which occur during each long cycle—one during each intermediate cycle. These serious contractions, unlike the more mild recessions such as that of 1953 or 1967, generate enough pessimism so that they are followed by a period of economic growth, i.e., another intermediate cycle. The first two of these serious contractions mark the intermediate cycles of the expansionary phase of our long cycle. They serve as smaller lessons of pain and help to reduce the cost of capital and labor, thus encouraging a resumption of the larger cyclical economic expansion. The next three of these serious contractions occur during the depressionary phase. The first of these marks the beginning of a massive liquidation and a deflation in expectations which extends through the next two serious contractions.

It is these intermediate cycles—or smaller boom-bust periods—which are the impetus for our long bull and bear markets. In the past, the three intermediate cycles occurring during the expansionary phase of the long cycle have been accompanied by a long, three-stage rise in stock prices. On the other hand, the two intermediate cycles occurring during the depressionary phase of the long cycle have provided only a one-stage bull market followed by a long decline in stock prices. Before we attempt to show how we can profit from these broad bull and bear markets, let us see how these intermediate cycles are affected by the political factor.

SIX

THE POLITICAL FACTOR AND THE ECONOMY

During seven of the last eight serious contractions, the most recent of which occurred in 1973–1974, people lost faith in the party controlling the White House. As it became apparent that the incumbent President could not handle the deteriorating economic conditions, we voted his party out of office shortly thereafter—usually in the following election. (See Table 6-1.) However, after the serious contractions of 1907, when the bankers were held more responsible than the government for the difficult times, and 1945, in which the contraction was less severe than the preceding one, two elections were necessary before the "ins" were thrown out. The only serious contraction that did not lead to a loss of faith and a subsequent change in the governing party was that of 1937–1938, which was not so severe as the one preceding it. In this case, as we had already lost confidence during the major depression of the early 1930s, we were not expecting very much.[1]

So, early in an intermediate cycle a different political party gains the White House. And there is a difference in its approach to the economy. The Democrats have traditionally believed that the econ-

---

[1]Conversely, the only change of a political party that did not follow a serious contraction was in 1968 when the Democrats were voted out of office. In this case, the social problems that crop up in times of exceedingly high economic expectations were at least partially responsible. We hoped that the Republicans would be able to slow things down.

TABLE 6-1   THE EFFECT OF SERIOUS ECONOMIC CONTRACTIONS ON PRESIDENTIAL ELECTIONS

Beginning of serious contraction	Loss of faith*	Following election
January 1893	May 1893	1896, Republicans capture White House: McKinley, Roosevelt-Taft administrations
May 1907	September 1907	1908, Republicans keep White House; lose it in 1912: Wilson administration
January 1920	May 1920	1920, Republicans capture White House: Harding-Coolidge-Hoover administrations
August 1929	December 1929	1932, Democrats win White House: Roosevelt administration
May 1937	September 1937	1940, Democrats keep White House: Roosevelt-Truman administrations
February 1945	June 1945	1948, Democrats keep White House; lose it in 1952: Eisenhower administration
May 1960	September 1960	1960, Democrats capture White House: Kennedy-Johnson administrations†
November 1973	March 1974	1976, Democrats capture White House: Carter administration

*Loss of faith begins approximately four months after contraction begins.

†Followed by a Republican administration: Nixon-Ford.

omy benefits most by increasing the purchasing power of the "little guys," such as laborers, farmers, and older people.[2] Given this philosophy, Democratic administrations traditionally favor programs to create and maintain jobs; letting business and the well-to-do carry the burden of the tax load; and providing subsidies to the needy, such as social security, food stamps, and price supports for the farmer. Of course, such a platform has led to a rise in government spending and big budget deficits which, in turn, have an inflationary effect on the economy. As a consequence, Democratic administrations have been more likely to influence wage and price decisions.

The Republicans, on the other hand, feel that their most important goal is to provide a favorable climate, i.e., a moderate tax load and stable prices, so that businesspeople will be encouraged to increase their capital formation.[3] As a result of this philosophy, Republican administrations have usually attempted to cut government spending; to lower taxes, especially for businesses; and to prevent inflation, perhaps at all costs.

Which of these approaches works? They both do—for a while, that is! Business executives responded to the cut in their taxes and reduced government spending that occurred during the Eisenhower administration by increasing their capital spending, which, in turn, propelled substantial advances in the level of employment and living standards. And the Democrats, when they took over in 1961, fostered programs to lower the level of unemployment, increased government spending, and cut taxes. As a result, total purchasing power was increased, providing the ammunition for the consumer buying spree that fueled the vigorous expansion of the 1960s.

What happens is that each of these approaches works because of the legacy that is inherited from the other party. The Roosevelt-Truman administrations, like other Democratic administrations, left

---

[2]The idea is that as these people increase their spending, we get increased business profits which, in turn, induce business managers to increase their spending for capital items. The result is a prosperity in which everyone benefits.

[3]The idea is that this increased business spending leads to more workers being hired and wages being boosted, so that, again, everyone benefits! This is called the "trickle down" theory.

a legacy of expanded consumer purchasing power.[4] During the following Republican administration, the consumer was able to keep up with the brisk expansion in capacity. Continued purchasing induced further business expansion and higher wages which, in turn, led to even higher spending. The result was a vigorous expansion.[5]

The Eisenhower administration, like the other Republican administrations, provided a legacy of lower government spending (during Eisenhower's eight years in office, federal spending fell from 15% to 10% of the gross national product), a lessening rate of inflation, and a goodly amount of unused resources. This legacy gave the subsequent Democratic administration plenty of room to expand the level of consumer purchasing power and government spending without igniting inflation. Once this occurred, the economy did pick up steam.

Yet, the problem is that each party pushes its approach too far—concentrating too much on one sector, either big business or the little guy, and neglecting the other. The initial success of its programs, in providing us with a prospering economy, leads to an easy reelection and what the party perceives as a mandate for its policies. Since adverse economic conditions led to the defeat of Herbert Hoover in 1932, each newly incumbent President has used the economic ammunition available to him—the most important tools being government spending and the size of the budget deficit—to help ensure that the period prior to the next election is a time of

---

[4]Even the Wilson administration took a favorable position toward labor and helped the farmers.

[5]At the present, some people are wondering if Carter, in his strong anti-inflation stance and pursuit of a balanced budget by 1981, is acting like a traditional Democrat. Yet, many of his programs, such as job creation and energy policy, and his attempt to let the burden of the increase in social security fall on business, show the traditional Democratic bias. We must remember that many harbored the same thoughts concerning Nixon, questioning whether he was a true Republican, when they saw him institute wage and price controls and expand the level of government spending. However, after his reelection, Nixon reversed course. He dismantled the wage and price controls, sharply reduced the government deficit, and showed a greater concern about inflation—all of which follow the traditional Republican dogma.

vigorous economic expansion.[6] With the reelection of the incumbent President, some of the more zealous members of the party are carried into office and the pressure to push the party's policies further mounts. Democratic administrations usually push their preoccupation with government spending and high employment, along with a tolerance to accept inflation, too far. Yet, as the Treasury's heavy borrowing makes it difficult to finance the investments needed to expand production, supplies cannot keep pace with the boosts in consumption. Each period of Democratic reign has ended with a towering rise in the rate of inflation and a relative falloff in the rate of capital formation. It is then necessary to bring the Republicans back into office so that the inflation can be cooled and a more sympathetic ear provided to businesspeople.

Republican administrations, on the other hand, usually go too far in cutting government spending, tolerating unemployment, and

---

[6]In fact, since 1932, the 18-month period prior to each election, except for 1960 when a contraction began shortly before the election, has been a time of vigorous business expansion. The election of 1960 was the only time that the incumbent President was barred by law from running again. Even more significant is the fact that a fairly important bottom in the stock market has been made anywhere from 7 to 23 months after each of these elections. This is no doubt due to the withdrawal of the stimulus just prior to or after the election. From these bottoms, the stock market advanced until the following election, as another round of stimulus was applied.

Bottom made	DJIA	December	DJIA	% gain
October 1933	83	1936	179	115
March 1938	98	1940	131	34
April 1942	92	1944	152	65
October 1946	163	1948	177	9
June 1949	161	1952	291	80
September 1953	255	1956	499	95
October 1957	419	1960	615	47
June 1962	535	1964	874	65
October 1966	744	1968	943	25
May 1970	631	1972	1020	60
December 1974*	577	1976	1004	75

*The December 1974 low was a one-day break of the October low of 584.

fighting inflation, and this effort leads to a deficiency in aggregate demand. Total consumer purchasing power is not able to keep pace with the brisk expansion in capital investment. At the end of each Republican reign, supplies have mounted and we get a serious contraction. It is then necessary to call in the Democrats so that they can expand consumer purchasing power.[7]

How long do a new political party's policies work before they lead to a serious contraction? Let us review what happened during the Nixon-Ford eight-year reign.

The Nixon administration came into office in 1969 and immediately began to apply a policy of modest economic restraint in order to break the inflation that it had inherited. This policy of modest restraint was abandoned during the ensuing recession in mid-1970, when sharply falling stock prices were threatening to undermine confidence; now Nixon began to increase government spending. However, in mid-1971, with the next election drawing nearer, the economy was still displaying a lack of vigor. With inflation still a problem, there was a fear that an additional stimulus would set off an inflationary spiral. It was at this time that Richard Nixon dropped his Republican dogma, instituted wage and price controls, undertook a huge budget deficit, and coaxed the Federal Reserve Board to increase money supply.[8] The result of these actions was that voters went to the polls in 1972 in the midst of a vigorous expansion, which did not hurt Nixon's prospects for reelection.

Yet, by late 1972, this expansion was becoming too vigorous in many areas; for example, agricultural prices, one of the few unrestricted areas of the economy, were skyrocketing.[9] Bottlenecks and shortages were appearing. It became obvious that a great deal of inflationary potential—suppressed for the moment by the price controls—was being built into the economy. If the administration hoped to avoid a disastrous inflation, the stimulus had to be withdrawn. So,

---

[7]This switch of party seems to be necessary. When it was delayed after the 1908 contraction, it was difficult to generate an expansion which lasted. Within a 59-month period, we got 47 months of recession (see Chart 5 in Chapter 5).

[8]The Fed's independence, which has been threatened by Congress, it seems, is dependent upon presidential support.

[9]Price controls had not been applied to the agricultural sector.

after his reelection, Nixon reverted to the traditional Republican dogma. Government spending was slowed, the budget swung from a huge deficit of $24 billion in fiscal 1972 to only a $4 billion deficit in fiscal 1974. Also, the Fed began reining in the money-supply growth and raising the discount rate. Shortly after this stimulus was pulled away from the rapidly growing economy, a contraction began—and became serious.

This period of initial prosperity, followed by increasing economic difficulties, was similar to what has taken place during each new reign of a political party. However, there is a difference, depending upon whether or not the party is the majority party. In the days of laissez faire economics, the Republicans dominated the federal government—the White House and Congress. In 1940, the Democrats won their third election in a row and became the majority party.[10] The age of the welfare state and the mixed economy[11] began. By and large, the majority party is more in tune with the particular phase of the industrial revolution that we are currently going through; that is the reason why it is the majority party. For our purposes, a party becomes the majority party when it first wins three elections in a row; a minority party does not hold the White House for more than eight consecutive years.

Naturally, the majority party has had an easier time of things than Nixon did and does not run into trouble until after its second reelection. The serious contraction has come after this reelection, e.g., in 1907 and 1929. However, when the majority party lost this second possible reelection in 1968, the change in economic emphasis was able to delay the serious contraction until after the reelection of the minority party. (See Table 6-2.)

In the case of a minority party, as it is not in tune with the basic direction of the industrial revolution, a serious contraction began *before* its second try at reelection. A serious contraction occurred in 1937 and 1973 just after the minority party's first try at reelection. This was due to the fact that a serious contraction had not occurred

---

[10]Even though the Republicans have held the White House for 16 of the last 28 years, in only 2 of these years did they hold majorities in Congress.

[11]In many instances, the market mechanism for resource allocation was replaced by government action.

TABLE 6-2   PRESIDENTIAL REELECTIONS AS RELATED TO SERIOUS ECONOMIC CONTRACTIONS

Party achieving White House	Second reelection	Serious contraction began in
MAJORITY PARTY		
1896 R	1904	1907
1920 R	1928	1929
1960 D	1968	lost election of 1968
1976 D	1984?	
MINORITY PARTY		
1912 D	1920	1920*
1932 D†	1940	1937‡
1952 R	1960	1960*
1968 R	1976	1973‡

R = Republican; D = Democratic.

*Serious contraction ran its course during prior reign.

†When the Democrats won in 1940, they became the majority party. Prior to that, they were still the minority party.

‡Serious contraction had not run its course during prior reign.

and run its course—that is, a subsequent expansion began—before the minority party came to power. On the other hand, in 1920 and in 1960, the serious contraction occurred shortly before the minority party's second try at reelection. In these two cases, a serious contraction had run its course during the majority party's prior reign. Thus the minority party had a somewhat easier time.

By looking at conditions from a political perspective, we can help pinpoint six of the last seven serious contractions. These contractions occurred either shortly before or after a political party's second try at reelection.

So, then, in the past, following a serious contraction, we got a change in political party and a consequent new approach in dealing with the economy. This new approach worked for a while and helped foster a period of economic growth. However, it soon led to an overheated economy followed by another serious contraction, which in turn led to this party's being thrown out of office. Another party arrived on the scene and then presided over a period of economic growth.

SEVEN

WHEN TO BUY AND SELL

Buy when the streets are running with blood.
BARON ROTHSCHILD, about 1815

Generally, the best time to buy stocks is during (or shortly after) a serious economic contraction when an important prior low in the stock market is broken.[1] Once that point is breached, many investors become frightened and seek an explanation of why support failed to materialize: that is, why other investors did not jump at the chance to buy stocks as this point was again approached. Of course, what they discover is that economic conditions have been deteriorating. An army of weary investors, or so it seems, become disillusioned and liquidate stocks that were bought when optimism was rampant. In this atmosphere of fear and gloom, a bottom in the stock market is soon made—generally within three months of the break of an important prior low (see Chart 6).

As investors have turned pessimistic and are discounting the worst that can happen—that is, they sold because they were expecting even worse economic news—bad news no longer brings out a rash of new stock liquidation. Nor is there a great deal of stock for sale which overhangs the market. Most people who wanted to sell have already done so. Thus, the market recovers when bargain hunters attempt to buy stocks. And this market recovery is soon followed by a significant improvement in the economy. This upturn occurs because businesspeople had also been affected by the widespread pessimism and had liquidated inventories, reduced debt, and

---

[1]An important low, by our definition, follows a five-year high. It is the lowest price in at least 18 months, and holds for a year or more before being broken (see Chart 4).

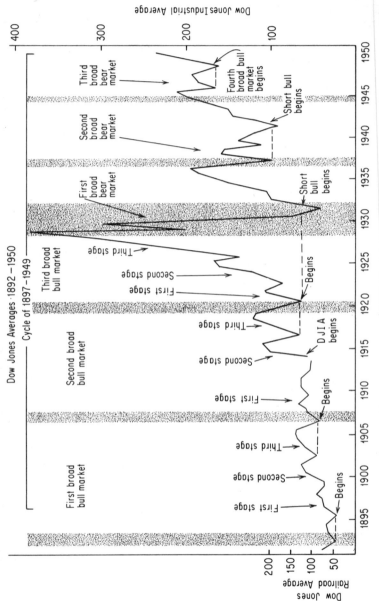

CHART 6a EACH BROAD BULL MARKET BEGAN WHEN A PRIOR LOW WAS BROKEN AND CONTAINED THREE STAGES WHICH WERE SEPARATED BY A BREAK OF 15% OR MORE. In Charts a and b, serious contractions are shaded. In Charts c–h, mild contractions are light-shaded while serious contractions are dark-shaded. In each of these charts, the 20-stock average was used for the period 1892–1897; the railroad average was used for the period 1897–1914; the industrial average was used for the period 1915 through the present.

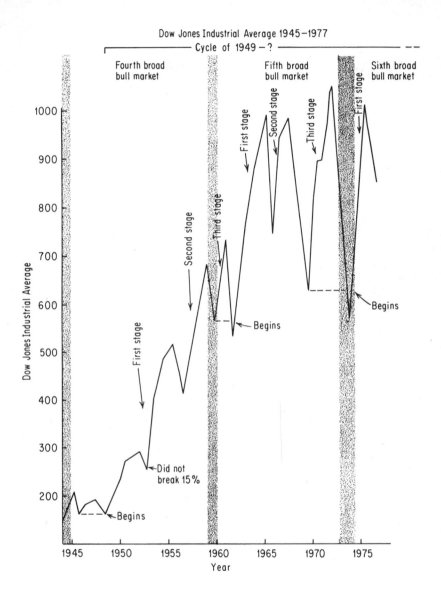

Dow Jones Industrial Average 1945–1977

CHART 6*b*.

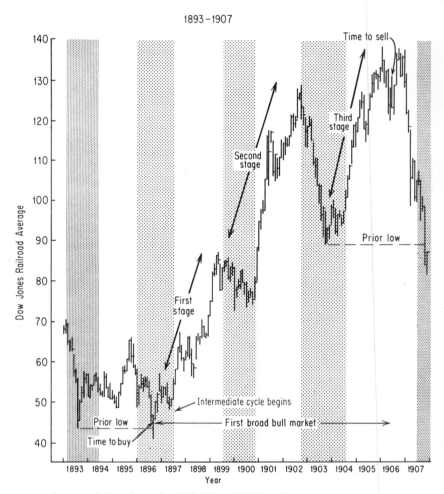

1893–1907

Dow Jones Railroad Average (monthly); Prior to 1897 20 stock average used.

SOURCE: Dow Jones Averages 1885–1970

CHART 6c   FIRST BROAD BULL MARKET.

delayed capital spending. The resulting lower business costs, along with a reduced stock of capital goods, provide a basis for rising earnings which, in turn, help fuel another bull market in stocks.

The time when we begin buying stocks depends mostly upon what has happened to long-term interest rates during the six months preceding the break of the important low. The long-term rate of

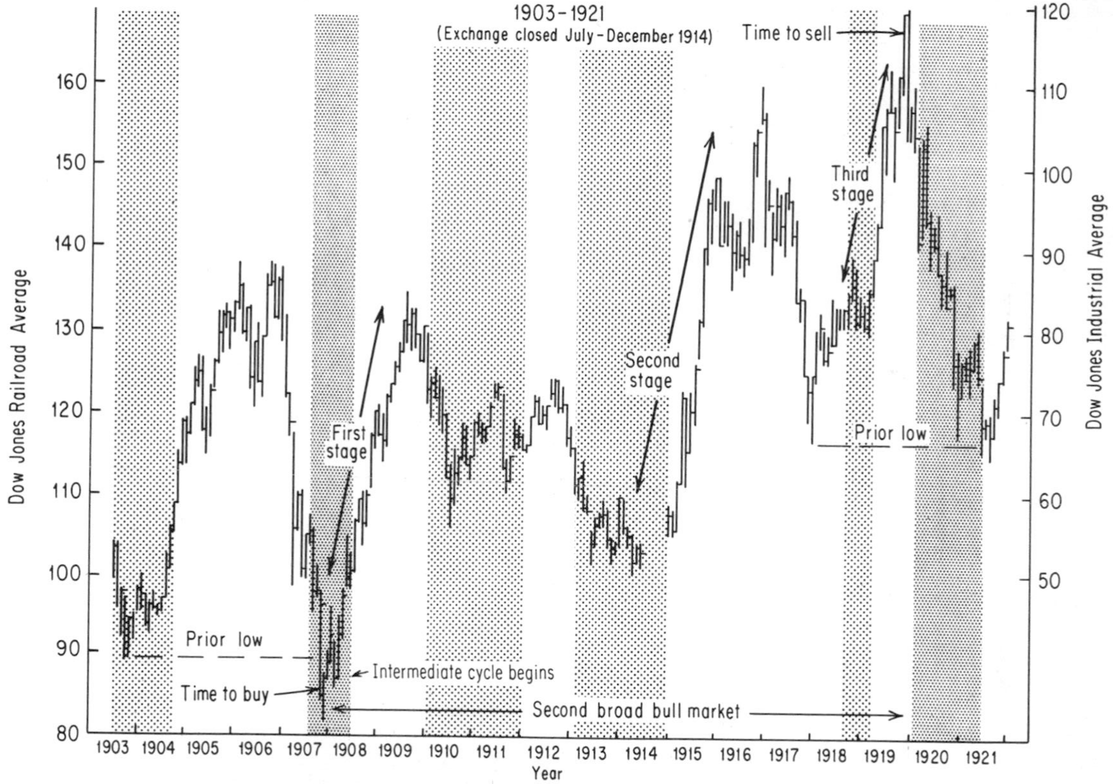

Dow Jones Industrial Average

Dow Jones Railroad Average

1903 – 1921
(Exchange closed July – December 1914)

Time to sell

Third stage

Second stage

First stage

Prior low

Time to buy

Intermediate cycle begins

Second broad bull market

Prior low

Year

Dow Jones Railroad Average until 1915 – Dow Jones Industrial Average 1915 – 1921 (monthly)
SOURCES: Dow Jones Averages 1885 – 1970

CHART 6d SECOND BROAD BULL MARKET.

85

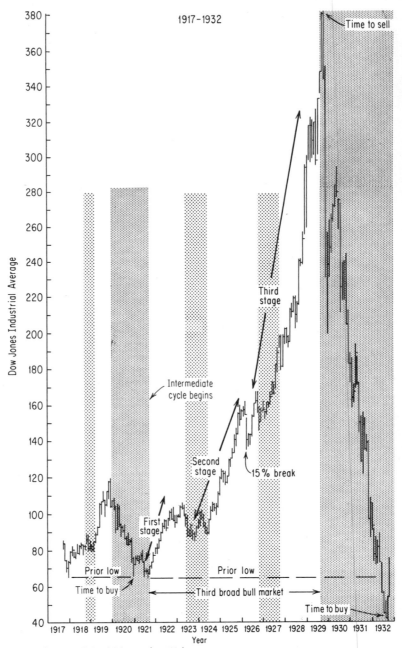

1917–1932

Time to sell

Third stage

Intermediate cycle begins

Second stage

15% break

First stage

Prior low · Prior low

Time to buy

Third broad bull market

Time to buy

Dow Jones Industrial Average (monthly)
SOURCE: Dow Jones Averages 1885-1920

CHART 6e   THIRD BROAD BULL MARKET.

Three Broad Bear Markets during Depressionary Phase:1929-1949

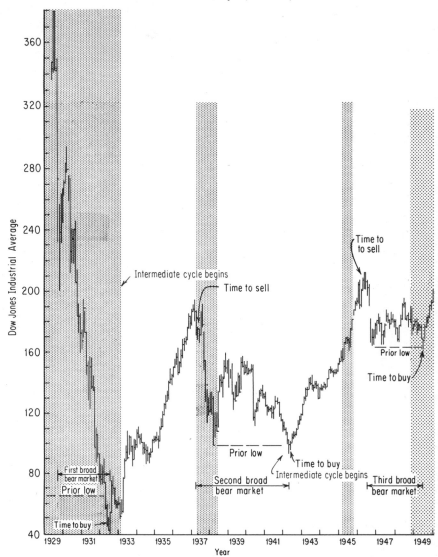

Dow Jones Industrial Average (monthly)
SOURCE: Dow Jones Averages 1885-1920

CHART 6f.

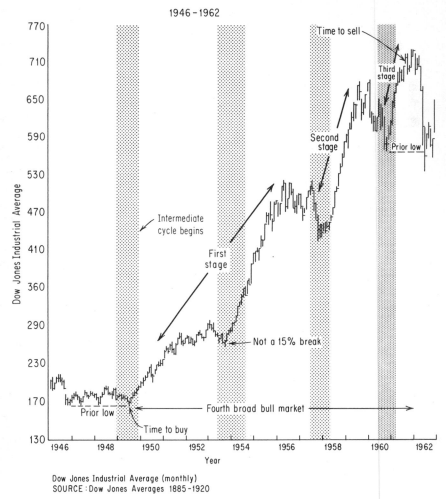

1946-1962

Dow Jones Industrial Average (monthly)
SOURCE: Dow Jones Averages 1885-1920

CHART 6g   FOURTH BROAD BULL MARKET.

interest, because it reflects whether people are extending or reducing their economic commitments, as we saw earlier, gives a good
indication of whether or not these people have begun to recognize
the worsening economic conditions. So, when the long-term rate of
interest has fallen during the six months preceding the break of the
important low in the stock market—that is, when long-term rates

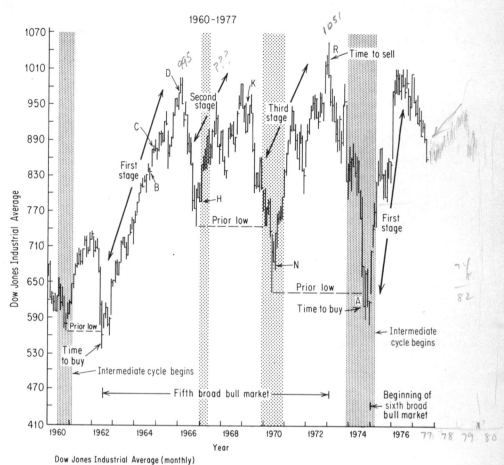

1960-1977

CHART 6*h* FIFTH BROAD BULL MARKET.

Dow Jones Industrial Average (monthly)
SOURCES: Dow Jones Averages 1885–1970; Dow Jones Investors Handbook 1971–1977

have made a new one-year low during that time[2] (see Table 7-5)—we can assume a sizable number of the public have recognized the poor economic prospects and have already sold stocks. In this case, we can expect that the liquidation of stocks will have run its course

---

[2]In the past, this has proved to be a reliable indication of how much longer we could expect the decline in the stock market to continue.

soon after the break of the prior low. The best time to buy stocks then seems to be three days after the second close of the DJIA (one day being too marginal) under the prior low.

On the other hand, when the long-term rate of interest has risen during the six months preceding the break of the important low without rates having made a one-year low during that time, we can assume that many people have not recognized that business conditions have worsened and have not yet sold stocks. Thus, we can expect that the liquidation of stocks still has some time to go. In this case, the best time to buy appears to be at the end of the second month following the second close under the important low: that is, at the end of June if the bottom came in April.

The last time we broke an important prior low was during the serious contraction of 1973–1975. In September 1974, the Dow broke its low of 631 that had been established in 1970. Yet, as long-term interest rates had not made a one-year low during the preceding six months, we should have waited until the end of November

TABLE 7-1   BREAKING AN IMPORTANT PRIOR LOW DURING OR SHORTLY AFTER A SERIOUS CONTRACTION *(Dow Jones Industrial Averages)*

Lows which were broken		Buy			Subsequent low
1893	43*	a Aug.	1896	43	—
1903	88*	b Dec.	1907	42†	41
1917	65	b Aug.	1921	67	66
1921	63	b June	1932	42	41
1938	98	a April	1942	96	92
1946	163	a June	1949	163	—
1960	566	a June	1962	536	535
1970	631	b Nov.	1974	618	577

a Interest rates made a one-year low during the preceding six months, bought three days after the second close under the prior low.

b Interest rates did not make a one-year low during the preceding six months, bought at the end of the second month following the break of the prior low.

*Rails.

†Approximate equivalent of the new Dow Jones Industrial Average which was introduced in December 1914.

before buying. The Dow, at that time, was 618, and five trading days later, it made a bottom at 577, just 7% below the level we would have bought at. It then began a major advance which carried it to 1014 by mid-1976. There have been seven other such major buying opportunities beginning with 1896 (the start of the last cycle) and including those in 1907, 1921, 1932, 1942, 1949, and 1962. Six occurred within eight trading days and 5% of the absolute bottom in the stock market; the other occurred just one and a half months and 10% after the bottom had been made.[3] (See Table 7-1.) Following each of these major bottoms, another bull market in stocks began.

Yet, the character of each of these bull markets is not the same. The reason is that the overriding psychology is different in expan-

---

[3]The only time the breaking of an important low did not occur during or shortly after a serious contraction was in 1970. That breaking occurred during the second recession of an intermediate cycle. Yet, even here, a fairly important bottom, one which held for over four years, was made soon after.

	Sold	% profit	Peak prior to next serious contraction	
128	May 1906	200	138*	Jan. 1906
118	Oct. 1919	185	119	Nov. 1919
380	Aug. 1929	460	381	Sept. 1929
174	April 1937	310	194	March 1937
212	May 1946	120	212	May 1946
705	July 1961	335	734	Dec. 1961
955	Feb. 1973	80	1051	Jan. 1973

sionary times than in depressionary times, and it affects people's willingness to extend their economic commitments. During expansionary times, people are experiencing an overriding psychology of increasing optimism and are willing to extend their economic commitments. We have gotten long three-staged bull markets which continue until overoptimism is achieved. During the depressionary phase, contrary to what many people may believe, we also experience bull markets which, in this case, reflect the improvement in business that occurs at the beginning of an intermediate cycle. However, as we are experiencing an overriding psychology of increasing pessimism wherein people are unwilling to extend their economic commitments, these bull markets contain only one stage. Thus, the character of the smaller cycles, such as bull and bear markets, is based on the phase of the larger cycle in which we are.

During the expansionary phase of the economic cycle, we get three stages in the stock market before the public loses its pessimism and becomes overoptimistic. In the past, each stage consisted of an advance in stock prices to their highest level in at least the last 27 months, and each stage was separated by a stock market break that corresponded to a business contraction. As business activity falters, some investors remember the sharp fall in stock prices that occurred during the last serious contraction and liquidate their holdings. However, many people, having witnessed the improvement in business conditions since the last serious contraction and having not yet bought, use this break to buy stocks. As a result, this break does not become a major one. While each of the breaks that occurred within the five broad bull markets were more than 15%,[4] only five exceeded 20%, and of these just two were more than 33%.[5] (See Chart 6.)

Just as the economic cycle proceeds from pessimism to mild optimism to excessive enthusiasm, so do these stages in the stock market. In the first stage of the bull market people are still influenced by the bad times just experienced. The public is skeptical and the market in general is underpriced. As a result, there are many good

---

[4]The only recession not accompanied by a stock market break of 15% or more was the mild recession of 1953; the first stage of the bull market ended with the second recession of the intermediate cycle, when stock prices fell by more than 15%.

[5]The record shows 40% in 1917 and 36% in 1969–1970.

values at this time. By the second stage, the Dow Jones Industrial Average makes a new all-time high and an increasing number of people begin to recognize the favorable economic prospects and start buying stocks, though cautiously. And, there is a shift in popularity from the blue chips, such as General Motors, Du Pont, and U.S. Steel, to the growth stocks, such as IBM, McDonald's, and Xerox. People have become more confident and therefore more willing to pay the premiums that stocks offering superior rates of growth command.

In the third stage, the stock market makes new highs. People get the message of a booming economy and once again lose their cautiousness. As a spreading euphoria colors their perceptions, people think that we are on the brink of perpetual prosperity and bid up the prices of unseasoned stocks to ridiculous heights, for they expect that soon the improving business conditions will justify such prices. (In January of 1973, at the top of the last broad bull market, *Barron's* printed the conclusions of its annual year-end panel, consisting of 10 so-called stock market experts, under the heading "Not a Bear among Them." Their modest expectation for 1973 was 1200 on the Dow!)

Yet, things are not what they seem. Just as too much pessimism establishes the conditions for a significant improvement in business together with a long rise in the value of assets, overoptimism sets up the conditions for a serious contraction *along with a severe break in the stock market.* Of the five breaks that followed these five broad bull markets, four were over 40% and the other was over 25% (see Table 7-1). And each of these breaks was *greater* than those coming at the end of the two preceding stages.

Thus, the time to leave the crowd and sell is during the third stage of the bull market. In the broad bull markets that have occurred since 1896, the time to sell has depended upon two things. If the stock market has already surpassed its high made during the second stage, then the time to sell has been at the end of the twenty-first month of the corresponding business expansion. This occurred in May 1906 and August 1929.

On the other hand, if, by the twenty-first month of the corresponding business expansion the stock market has not surpassed its high made during the second stage, then the time to sell is at the end of the third month following a new all-time high in the stock market. This point in time occurred in October 1919, July 1961, and February 1973. It appears that by these times enough of the public has gotten the message of a booming economy and bought stocks, so that an expanding economy is no longer able to induce the level of new stock buying necessary to fuel this bull market. Thus, the best time to sell during the third stage of a bull market is either 21 months into the corresponding business expansion or at the end of the third month after the Dow exceeds the high made during the second stage—*whichever comes later* (Chart 6). Each of these selling times occurred within four and a half months and 9% of the top in the stock market (see Table 7-1). In each case, people who sold then would have missed the brunt of the following stock market break.

Accordingly, we can redefine bull markets. What are commonly thought of as single bull markets, such as occurred in 1949–1953 and 1962–1966, are actually stages in broader bull markets. And what we thought of as bear markets in 1953, 1957, and 1966, for example, are actually abortive bears or interruptions of a broader bull market.

During the depressionary phase of the cycle, bull markets are not broad. They contain a single stage and do not achieve the level of optimism experienced in expansionary times. In the two one-stage bull markets that occurred during the last depressionary phase, the best time to sell was during the first expansion of the intermediate cycle, after long-term interest rates had risen by 10%,[6] thus signaling that people had extended their economic commitments too much. If, however, interest rates have not risen by this amount during the first expansion of the intermediate cycle, then the time to sell is seven months after the second expansion of the intermediate cycle begins. At this time, stock prices have gone about as far as they are likely to. Both these selling times would have occurred within two months and 10% of the top in the stock market (Chart 6,).

This one-stage bull market is followed by a long decline in stock prices. After the sharp break that occurs during the serious contraction, there is a rally—associated with a new business expansion—

---

[6]The appropriate time to sell is at the end of the month in which this rise occurs.

TABLE 7-2 DOW JONES INDUSTRIAL AVERAGES

Bear market	At beginning	Low of first stage	Rally high	Retraced	Low of second stage
1929–1932	381	198	294	51%	41
1937–1942	194	98	158	56%	92
1946–1949	212	163	193	52%	161

which retraces only slightly more than one-half the preceding break of the DJIA (see Table 7-2). From the point of the rally high, a second-stage down begins and continues until the low made during the serious contraction is broken. This break of the prior low means that investors have gotten the message that poor business conditions are in prospect. Yet, again, things are not what they seem and a new buying opportunity is occurring.

The exception was the bear market of 1929–1933, which was the beginning of the depressionary phase of the cycle. In this case, when the prior low of 1929 was taken out, the break accelerated and continued until the low of 63, made at the beginning of the intermediate cycle, was broken. Of course, the low of 1929 was not an important low. But, even if it had been, we could have expected a long decline to follow, as people were losing confidence and reducing their economic commitments. The beginning of the depressionary phase of the cycle is the one time when the stock market may not be able to make a major bottom soon after breaking a prior low.

Accordingly, we can redefine bear markets. Thus, what were thought to be single bear markets, such as occurred in 1937–1938 and 1939–1941, were really stages in a broader bear market, which was interrupted by the rally of 1938–1939.

Yet, how do we know the phase of the long cycle in which we are? The expansionary phase typically consists of three intermediate cycles, each of which contains a broad bull market wherein the stock market makes new all-time highs (see Chart 6). During the second of these intermediate cycles, the long-term rate of interest surpasses the natural rate of interest and remains above this natural rate during the third intermediate cycle, signaling that new investment is being added at a high level of fixed cost. By the end of the third intermediate cycle, that is, the third traditional business expansion of the intermediate cycle, we should be experiencing a great deal of optimism and speculative activity in both the stock market and the economy. The historical signs of overoptimism, such as a short interest ratio (monthly short interest as a ratio of average daily volume) below 1.10, are likely to be occurring in the stock market. This is the time to think seriously of abandoning economic commitments whether in stocks, real estate, or perhaps one's own business, as the depressionary phase of our long cycle, wherein the value of assets has a dramatic fall, is about to begin.

On the other hand, the depressionary phase typically contains two intermediate cycles, during which the stock market is unable to make a new all-time high. By the end of the second of these intermediate cycles, we should have experienced three broad bear markets and the long-term rate of interest should have fallen below the natural rate of interest, signaling that new investment could now be added at a low level of fixed cost (see Chart 6). Also by this time, business earnings are likely to have experienced a huge increase. In 1948, aggregate earnings of the stocks in the DJIA surpassed their level of 1929. This was a further sign that we were about to embark on a long period of expansion.

An investor who bought and sold in the manner described in this chapter would have bought near the bottom of the seven bull markets since 1896 (both the broad ones that occur in expansionary times and the short ones that we get in depressionary times) and sold near the top (see Table 7-1). In addition, the investor would have established a position early in the present bull market. And each time after selling out, the individual would have been able to buy back substantially lower—at least 23%. An investment of $1000 in 1921, approximately one long cycle ago, would be worth $5 million today! That is a compounded rate of return of approximately 17%. It is also way above what one can currently get on bonds and also above the results of the 1964 study by Lorie and Fischer (mentioned in Chapter 5).

In addition, we may develop a strategy to take advantage of the stock market breaks which are moderately severe—that is, when prices fall by more than 25%—and are occurring within a broad bull market. Of the five moderately severe breaks that occurred within the five broad bull markets, four were preceded by a rally in long-term interest rates to above the high made during the prior business expansion. We can take this rise in interest as a sign that people are overextending their economic commitments, including stocks, and that an economic contraction accompanied by a stock market break of some consequence will soon follow.[7]

However, a broad bull market is usually not vulnerable to a moderately severe break during the first two years in the life of its first and second stages. In the past, this vulnerability began at about the twenty-sixth month of those stages. If, by that time, long-term interest rates have exceeded their highs made during the previous business expansion, this was the time to reduce positions.[8] When this new high in long-term interest rates occurred after the twenty-sixth month, the time to reduce positions then was at the end of the month in which the high occurred (see Table 7-3).

In these cases, the best time to rebuy was shortly after either a 25% break[9] in the stock market or a sizable decline in long-term interest rates, whichever came first. The time to rebuy was at the end of the second month following a 25% break. However, if long-term interest rates had a sizable break—in the past an 8% break was sufficient—before the stock market had broken 25%, it meant that economic commitments had been reduced and the pressure was off the stock market. As such, a lesser break can occur. In this case, the time to

---

[7]Only 5 stock market breaks of 15% or more which occurred during the expansionary phase of the cycle—and 4 of the last 15 economic contractions which began during that time—were not preceded by such a rally in long-term interest rates; of these, 2 were less than 20%, another, in 1910–1912, was 28%; in the fourth case, preceding the 1973 top, interest rates were suppressed because of the government's price control program; and just recently as of November 1977, we have had a break of 21%.

[8]It is not wise to reduce equity positions beyond 50% during a long bull market. This is so because there is still upside potential so that any loss suffered by sitting through these breaks is likely to be soon made up. On the other hand, if we had sold too soon or after we sold, we had overestimated the extent of the decline, we could end up missing out on an important part of the price rise.

[9]In the past, only one break within a broad bull market, that of 1917, was materially more than 25%. This probably had to do with the fact that a break of this magnitude leads people to notice, just as we do at a fire sale, that prices have become relatively cheap.

TABLE 7-3   DOW JONES INDUSTRIAL AVERAGES

	First stage			
	Sell		Rebuy	
FIRST CYCLE				
First broad bull market				
Second broad bull market				
Third broad bull market				
SECOND CYCLE				
First broad bull market	270	Aug. 1951	280	Dec. 1953
	502	Aug. 1956	439	Feb. 1958†
Second broad bull market	969	Dec. 1965	785	Dec. 1966

*Dow Jones Railroad Average.

†There were two business expansions during this stage; in August of 1956 long-term interest rates went over the highs made during the first business expansion.

rebuy was at the end of the month following the 8% break in interest rates. In each case, it was best to go back to a fully invested position so that we would be able to participate fully in the following stage.[10] We can see the record of these transactions in Table 7-3. Had we followed such a plan, we would have bought back at a lower price (according to the averages) following six of the seven times we sold out.[11]

Let us now see how we would have fared through the broad bull market which began in 1962. We will start with $10,000 and will also take advantage of the shift in leadership from the blue chip to growth stocks which normally occurs about one year after the DJIA makes a new all-time high. We will use General Motors, the premier blue chip, and IBM, the leading growth stock, as our investment vehicles (see Table 7-4).

---

[10]This was also a good time for those who had not yet bought to enter the market— especially during the break following the first stage.

[11]During the long first stage of 1949–1956, we got two business expansions, and as long-term interest rates went over the high made during the preceding expansion both times, we would have reduced positions twice during this stage.

Second stage			Final stage
Sell		Rebuy	Final sale
127*	Aug. 1902	89*	Sept. 1903	128*	May 1906
102	Sept. 1916	72	Nov. 1917	118	Oct. 1919
	none			380	Aug. 1929
679	Dec. 1959	580	Sept. 1960	705	July 1961
943	Dec. 1968	683	June 1970	955	Feb. 1973

TABLE 7-4   AN EXAMPLE OF PURCHASES AND SALES BASED ON MARKET TRENDS AND INTEREST RATES

			Cost	Proceeds
Bought	6/25/62	217 shares of General Motors @ $45.50	$10,000	
Sold	9/30/64	217 shares of General Motors @ $99.25		$21,550
Bought	9-/30/64	186 shares of IBM @ $116	$21,550	
Sold	12/31/65	93 shares of IBM @ $134		$12,450
Bought	12/30/66	84 shares of IBM @ $148	$12,450	
Sold	12/31/68	88 shares of IBM @ $255		$22,450
Bought	6/30/70	111 shares of IBM @ $202	$22,450	
Sold	2/28/73	200 shares of IBM @ $353		$70,600
Bought	11/29/74	2315 shares General Motors @ $30.50	$70,600	
Value	12/31/76			$177,900

After having sold out in July 1961, the third month after the stock market surpassed its high made during the second stage of the broad bull market, with the Dow at 705, we would have waited on the sidelines for the sign that a new broad bull market was about to begin. This occurred in June of 1962, when the important low of 1960 at 566 in the Dow was broken.

On June 25, three days after the second close under the prior low—as long-term interest rates had made a new yearly low in May at 4.28% (see Table 7-5), within six months of this break—we would have bought with the Dow at 536. In this case, our $10,000 entitled us to 217 shares of General Motors, which was then selling at $45½ a share. On the following day, the Dow made a bottom at 535 and began a three-staged advance which was to last until January 1973. The first stage lasted 44 months, until February of 1966, and saw the Dow hit 995. As long-term interest rates were still well below the highs made during the preceding business expansion in August of 1964, the twenty-sixth month in the life of the first stage of this bull market, we would have done nothing (Chart 6, point B). However, by the following month, September, one year had passed since the Dow had made a new all-time high. So, on September 30, we would have switched from General Motors to IBM (Chart 6, point C). We would have sold our General Motors at $99.25 a share and applied the proceeds of $21,550 to buy 186 shares of IBM at a price of $116 per share.[12]

The first sign of impending trouble appeared in December 1965, when long-term interest rates bettered their highs of 4.65% made during the preceding expansion (Chart 6, point D). This rise meant that we could expect a moderately severe break in the stock market. However, as we were still in the early part of a broad bull market, we would have sold only one-half of our position, or 93 shares of our IBM at $134 a share. This sale would have netted us $12,450. During the following 10 months, the stock market broke 25%. The Dow, which was 969 when we sold, was 785 on December 30, 1966, the end of the second month following the 25% break (Chart 6, point H). This fact would seem to justify the reduction in our position. How-

---

[12]Adjusted for the 5 for 4 split in 1964, the 3 for 2 split in 1966, the 2 for 1 split in 1968, and the 5 for 4 split in 1973.

ever, as IBM had bucked the trend and was selling at $148 at the time we were ready to rebuy, our $12,480 would have allowed us to buy back only 84 of the 93 shares we had sold. In this case, reducing our position would have been a frustrating experience.

The second stage began in October 1966 and lasted exactly 26 months. And, just nine months into this stage, in July of 1967, long-term interest rates exceeded their high made during the preceding business expansion. This rise meant that we were to reduce our position at the end of the twenty-sixth month in the life of this stage, or on December 31, 1968, with the Dow at 943 (Chart 6, point K). In this case, we would have netted $22,450 by selling 88 shares of IBM at $258 a share—one-half our position. During the following year and a half, we got a moderately severe break in the stock market—the Dow fell 36%—which accompanied the second contraction of the intermediate cycle. Yet, as we had another stage of this broad bull market coming, as well as a third business expansion before we got our serious contraction, we bought on June 30, 1970, the end of the second month following the 25% break in the stock market, with the Dow at 683 (Chart 6, point N). This was also the end of the second month following the break of the 1966 low, which again suggested a fairly important bottom.[13] In this case, our $22,450 would have entitled us to another 111 shares of IBM at $202 a share. This purchase occurred just five weeks after, and at 8% above, the low in the Dow. Here, reducing our position was justified.

The third stage of this bull market began in May 1970 and continued until the Dow had reached 1051. It is during this stage that a top in the stock market occurs. In this case, the Dow had not bettered its high made during the second stage by the twenty-first month of the third business expansion of the intermediate cycle. Consequently, the time to sell would have been at the end of the third month after the Dow had made a new high. The Dow closed over its high of 985, made during the second stage, on November 9, 1972. Then, on February 28, 1973, the end of the third following month, with the Dow at 955, we would have sold our entire position: 200 shares of IBM at $353 a share, netting us $70,600 (Chart 6, point R). This was

---

[13]As this was coming during the second contraction of the intermediate cycle—not the serious contraction—it was not a major bottom.

TABLE 7-5 MONTHLY AVERAGE BOND YIELDS (PRIME CORPORATE), JANUARY 1900 THROUGH SEPTEMBER 1977

	Jan.	Feb.	March	April	May	June	July
1900	3.31	3.30	3.29	3.28	3.31	3.32	3.31
1901	3.26	3.25	3.24	3.25	3.28	3.27	3.29
1902	3.30	3.30	3.29	3.29	3.31	3.32	3.33
1903	3.43	3.45	3.49	3.52	3.51	3.55	3.59
1904	3.59	3.60	3.61	3.60	3.59	3.57	3.54
1905	3.51	3.50	3.50	3.51	3.52	3.51	3.51
1906	3.53	3.55	3.59	3.61	3.64	3.64	3.66
1907	3.77	3.80	3.85	3.85	3.87	3.90	3.90
1908	3.96	3.95	3.99	3.96	3.93	3.93	3.92
1909	3.79	3.77	3.78	3.78	3.77	3.78	3.77
1910	3.79	3.80	3.82	3.86	3.88	3.90	3.93
1911	3.89	3.90	3.91	3.91	3.90	3.91	3.91
1912	3.91	3.90	3.91	3.92	3.92	3.94	3.94
1913	3.99	4.00	4.07	4.12	4.16	4.21	4.21
1914	4.16	4.10	4.11	4.09	4.08	4.06	4.09
1915	4.17	4.15	4.19	4.14	4.15	4.19	4.25
1916	4.06	4.05	4.07	4.09	4.09	4.10	4.12
1917	3.98	4.05	4.10	4.19	4.32	4.36	4.41
1918	4.79	4.75	4.82	4.87	4.81	4.87	4.92
1919	4.71	4.75	4.79	4.83	4.77	4.76	4.80
1920	4.95	5.10	5.11	5.32	5.56	5.52	5.50
1921	5.13	5.17	5.23	5.26	5.29	5.42	5.28
1922	4.71	4.71	4.65	4.55	4.51	4.49	4.39
1923	4.39	4.61	4.54	4.58	4.52	4.56	4.58
1924	4.63	4.66	4.66	4.63	4.59	4.52	4.46
1925	4.51	4.50	4.48	4.47	4.42	4.43	4.47
1926	4.43	4.40	4.41	4.36	4.32	4.33	4.35
1927	4.30	4.30	4.26	4.21	4.19	4.23	4.23
1928	4.04	4.05	4.06	4.08	4.13	4.23	4.30
1929	4.38	4.42	4.46	4.46	4.48	4.53	4.56
1930	4.42	4.40	4.33	4.38	4.35	4.32	4.27
1931	4.10	4.10	4.10	4.08	3.99	4.01	4.00
1932	4.64	4.70	4.60	4.76	4.77	4.83	4.73
1933	4.14	4.15	4.32	4.49	4.34	4.18	4.11
1934	4.07	3.99	3.93	3.86	3.82	3.74	3.74
1935	3.57	3.50	3.46	3.45	3.46	3.43	3.40
1936	3.26	3.20	3.14	3.12	3.09	3.07	3.09
1937	2.97	3.08	3.21	3.25	3.20	3.17	3.15
1938	3.04	3.03	3.01	3.03	2.95	2.94	2.92
1939	2.75	2.75	2.74	2.75	2.71	2.71	2.69
1940	2.71	2.70	2.66	2.65	2.72	2.75	2.71
1941	2.66	2.65	2.63	2.64	2.61	2.58	2.54

August	Sept.	Oct.	Nov.	Dec.
3.31	3.32	3.32	3.29	3.27
3.31	3.32	3.32	3.30	3.30
3.35	3.37	3.40	3.41	3.43
3.64	3.64	3.60	3.58	3.59
3.53	3.55	3.55	3.54	3.53
3.51	3.51	3.51	3.53	3.54
3.69	3.72	3.73	3.73	3.75
3.95	3.99	4.06	4.21	4.10
3.88	3.85	3.85	3.83	3.81
3.77	3.78	3.79	3.80	3.80
3.92	3.88	3.86	3.89	3.89
3.93	3.94	3.94	3.92	3.92
3.96	3.98	3.98	3.98	3.99
4.17	4.13	4.17	4.23	4.24
				4.22
4.28	4.30	4.21	4.08	4.08
4.14	4.12	4.07	4.04	4.04
4.45	4.54	4.98	4.73	4.81
4.93	4.98	4.86	4.59	4.61
4.95	4.96	4.83	4.94	4.99
5.36	5.18	5.03	5.13	5.30
5.20	5.14	5.12	4.92	4.78
4.33	4.30	4.38	4.44	4.41
4.57	4.61	4.64	4.62	4.65
4.50	4.50	4.48	4.49	4.51
4.53	4.49	4.51	4.49	4.46
4.37	4.37	4.26	4.33	4.32
4.19	4.15	4.11	4.06	4.04
4.36	4.31	4.30	4.27	4.34
4.52	4.59	4.56	4.46	4.43
4.21	4.14	4.12	4.16	4.22
4.04	4.08	4.29	4.42	4.66
4.48	4.40	4.41	4.44	4.33
4.06	4.08	4.09	4.23	4.19
3.79	3.86	3.79	3.70	3.66
3.43	3.44	3.44	3.38	3.33
3.10	3.07	3.05	3.01	2.95
3.13	3.14	3.14	3.09	3.05
2.92	2.92	2.88	2.83	2.81
2.72	3.03	2.91	2.77	2.72
2.69	2.64	2.64	2.62	2.62
2.53	2.54	2.52	2.51	2.60

TABLE 7-5 (*Continued*)

	Jan.	Feb.	March	April	May	June	July
1942	2.62	2.65	2.67	2.63	2.63	2.63	2.61
1943	2.60	2.57	2.57	2.56	2.56	2.53	2.51
1944	2.57	2.56	2.55	2.54	2.54	2.53	2.52
1945	2.54	2.53	2.52	2.51	2.52	2.51	2.53
1946	2.46	2.39	2.38	2.37	2.41	2.41	2.41
1947	2.50	2.51	2.52	2.49	2.49	2.49	2.50
1948	2.82	2.82	2.81	2.75	2.74	2.75	2.82
1949	2.74	2.73	2.72	2.73	2.73	2.72	2.68
1950	2.57	2.58	2.59	2.61	2.62	2.63	2.65
1951	2.64	2.67	2.80	2.89	2.91	3.00	2.98
1952	3.04	3.00	3.03	3.00	3.00	3.00	3.03
1953	3.07	3.15	3.20	3.32	3.42	3.43	3.35
1954	3.11	3.00	2.91	2.91	2.94	2.96	2.96
1955	2.98	3.04	3.07	3.05	3.09	3.09	3.10
1956	3.13	3.09	3.09	3.21	3.28	3.26	3.27
1957	3.76	3.68	3.65	3.65	3.72	3.84	4.01
1958	3.67	3.61	3.65	3.63	3.59	3.59	3.68
1959	4.09	4.10	4.09	4.17	4.34	4.45	4.48
1960	4.60	4.55	4.46	4.42	4.46	4.47	4.40
1961	4.32	4.27	4.22	4.25	4.27	4.33	4.41
1962	4.42	4.42	4.39	4.33	4.28	4.28	4.34
1963	4.21	4.19	4.19	4.21	4.22	4.23	4.26
1964	4.37	4.36	4.38	4.40	4.41	4.41	4.40
1965	4.43	4.41	4.42	4.43	4.44	4.46	4.48
1966	4.74	4.78	4.92	4.96	4.98	5.07	5.16
1967	5.20	5.03	5.13	5.11	5.24	5.44	5.58
1968	6.17	6.10	6.11	6.21	6.27	6.28	6.24
1969	6.59	6.66	6.85	6.89	6.79	6.98	7.08
1970	7.91	7.93	7.84	7.83	8.11	8.48	8.44
1971	7.36	7.08	7.21	7.25	7.53	7.64	7.64
1972	7.19	7.27	7.24	7.30	7.30	7.23	7.21
1973	7.15	7.22	7.29	7.26	7.29	7.37	7.45
1974	7.83	7.85	8.01	8.25	8.37	8.47	8.72
1975	8.83	8.62	8.67	8.95	8.90	8.77	8.84
1976	8.60	8.55	8.52	8.40	8.58	8.62	8.56
1977	7.96	8.04	8.10	8.04	8.05	7.95	7.94

Source until 1961: *A History of Interest Rates*, second edition, by Sidney Homer, copyright © 1963, 1977 by Rutgers, the State University of New Jersey. Reprinted by permission of Rutgers University Press.

Source from 1961 to present: Federal Reserve Bulletin, Monthly Average.

August	Sept.	Oct.	Nov.	Dec.
2.61	2.60	2.61	2.59	2.61
2.52	2.54	2.53	2.54	2.58
2.53	2.55	2.56	2.58	2.56
2.55	2.54	2.53	2.54	2.54
2.43	2.50	2.53	2.53	2.56
2.50	2.56	2.66	2.74	2.82
2.87	2.85	2.85	2.85	2.81
2.63	2.62	2.62	2.59	2.59
2.61	2.65	2.66	2.65	2.66
2.91	2.89	2.94	3.02	3.06
3.03	3.03	3.07	3.03	3.01
3.33	3.38	3.23	3.15	3.19
2.94	2.98	2.95	2.95	2.96
3.16	3.19	3.14	3.13	3.16
3.60	3.40	3.59	3.68	3.74
4.17	4.23	4.22	4.20	3.91
3.87	4.09	4.16	4.12	4.08
4.44	4.52	4.65	4.57	4.57
4.23	4.22	4.30	4.29	4.31
4.45	4.45	4.42	4.39	4.42
4.35	4.32	4.28	4.25	4.24
4.29	4.31	4.32	4.33	4.35
4.41	4.42	4.42	4.43	4.44
4.49	4.52	4.56	4.60	4.68
5.31	5.49	5.41	5.35	5.39
5.62	5.65	5.82	6.07	6.19
6.02	5.97	6.09	6.19	6.45
6.97	7.14	7.33	7.35	7.72
8.13	8.09	8.03	8.05	7.64
7.59	7.44	7.39	7.26	7.25
7.19	7.22	7.21	7.12	7.08
7.68	7.63	7.60	7.67	7.68
9.00	9.24	9.27	8.89	8.89
8.95	8.95	8.86	8.78	8.79
8.45	8.38	8.32	8.25	7.98
7.98	7.92			

just one and a half months after, and 9% below, the final top of 1051 in the stock market. During the course of this broad bull market, while the Dow rose 96%, the smallest rise of the five broad bull markets, we made over 600% on our original investment, not including dividends. In addition, we had gotten out of the stock market and into cash just before the biggest stock market break in 36 years.

Had we then used this $70,600 to buy 2,315 shares of General Motors at $30½ a share on November 29, 1974, per our buy signal (when the Dow was 618, as shown at point A in Chart 6), our original $10,000 would have been worth $177,900 (not including dividends) by December of 1976—an increase of 1680% (Table 7-4). (That is a 22% compounded rate of return.) This gain contrasts with an increase of 87%, had an investor bought the stocks in the Dow Jones Industrial Average in June 1962, and then sat.

During each long economic cycle, we have gotten a repetitive series of broad bull and bear markets; three broad bull markets broken by brief bear markets and followed by three broad bear markets which are separated by only brief bull markets, all moving in the direction of the larger cycle. It is this variation, in which broad bull markets are not followed by real bear markets (those lasting for two or more stages) and real bear markets are not followed by broad bull markets, that is not accounted for by contemporary cycle theorists, such as those advocating the Dow Theory. Now, let us look further at which stocks to buy.

EIGHT

PICKING STOCKS

Each stock does not participate equally in the broad bull and bear markets. During the broad bull market extending from 1962 to 1968, Chrysler appreciated over 700% while, at the 1968 top, U.S. Steel sold only a bit more than 20% above its 1962 low. How do we come up with more Chryslers than U.S. Steels?

To begin, we need some basis for classifying stocks according to their similar characteristics, since there are too many stocks to handle separately. We generally recognize two important sectors in the stock market: the "blue chips," the leading companies in those industries that have established an important role within the structure of the American economy prior to the present expansionary period; and the speculatives, those companies that are now (in the present expansionary period) in the process of proving (or failing to prove) themselves. The part these speculative stocks are likely to play in the American economy is not yet clear. The speculative sector includes a growth segment, those companies of a new industry, such as computers in the late 1950s, and a low price segment, the marginal companies of an older industry, such as American Motors. Of the two, the growth segment is the more important to stock market profits; it is this segment of the speculative sector that will be discussed in this chapter.

The difference between blue chip and speculative stocks is in the risk that the players perceive. The blue chip sector, as it contains those companies that have already attained a record of past performance, such as Du Pont, General Motors, and U.S. Steel, is seen as the less risky vehicle to participate in America's ongoing prosperity. The risk of total or near total loss is assumed to be minimal. During the crisis of 1970, Penn Central was the only blue chip to go bankrupt, in contrast with a whole slew of speculative stocks, including Four Seasons, National Video, and King Resources, that went to near zero in price at that time.

Growth stocks, on the other hand, offer an opportunity to capitalize on those areas that are achieving a proportionally high level of growth. Their appeal is that their future earnings growth appears to be relatively unlimited. Unlike the market for the steels or papers, which are now mature industries, the potential market for the products of growth companies is relatively unexploited or is expanding. As a result, it is believed that these companies will be able to employ their retained earnings quite profitably, and the utilization of new capital is not likely to intensify or lead to overcapacity problems. Hence, they can probably sustain their earnings growth for a long period.

However, the potential of an IBM, McDonald's, or a Xerox, once it grows to a certain size, is likely to be recognized by many investors, so that the stock sells at a quite high premium from its current performance—or in stock market parlance, "on the basis of future expectations." Because of this premium, growth stocks often present a high degree of risk; that is, the loss is considerable when such a stock fails to live up to investor expectations. It is for this reason that growth stocks are considered speculative.

Of course, the sector to which a stock belongs may change. As time goes on, the leading growth stocks become blue chips. In the prior expansionary period, which extended from 1897 to 1929, most of the stocks which presently make up the Dow Jones Industrial Averages were then considered growth stocks. And the railroads, as they had already proven themselves, were considered the blue chips.

Investor favor tends to focus on one or the other of these sectors at different periods within a broad bull market. This is so because each of these sectors is seen as vulnerable to a different kind of risk. When perceptions of risk increase following a serious contraction, the blue chips—with their conservative pricing—are the stocks to own. They dominated throughout the first stage of the past two broad bull markets. The Dow Jones Industrial Average, which consists largely of today's blue chips, increased about 225% from 1949 until 1956, and again about 80% from 1962 until 1965. However, during this stage (usually about one year after the Dow Jones Industrial Averages have made a new high) the blue chips usually become overpriced, with their prices reflecting a rate of growth which a mature company cannot maintain. During the following recession (for example, 1957 and 1966), they undergo severe damage. When this happens, investors begin looking for those companies which are achieving superior rates of earnings growth—or the growth stocks.

The growth sector leads during the remainder of the broad bull market: IBM, the leading and most representative stock of this sector, rose over 375% from late 1957 to 1961, and again about 200% from late 1966 to 1973. (On the other hand, the Dow Jones Industrial Average rose only 75% and 40%, respectively, during these periods.) Growth stocks, as they more fully reflect the growth that occurs during the expansionary phase of the cycle, usually capture investor favor through two market stages (e.g., 1966–1968 and 1970–1973) of a broad bull market (see Chart 7). The first stage (1957–1959 or 1966–1968) is fueled by the growing recognition of these superior rates of growth. Then, following a market break associated with a recession (as in 1960 and 1970), the second stage begins wherein the potential earnings growth of this sector is overdiscounted. Heightened stock prices and earnings are likely to lead to unjustified assumptions, not only by investors, but also by management. Expansion is likely to be pushed too far and too fast at the same time that investors are bidding up the prices of these stocks. At this point, this sector is left particularly vulnerable.[1] As costs increase and competition intensifies, it becomes more and more difficult to live up to these high expectations. During the next market break (the one associated with a serious contraction), the growth stocks suffer huge losses and their decline in turn serves to alter the players' perceptions of risk. Investors become more cautious and begin favoring the blue chips once more. Thus, investor favor alternates between the

---

[1]As the cyclical expansion matures, one period of investor favor, as in 1926–1929, may be enough to fully discount their potential.

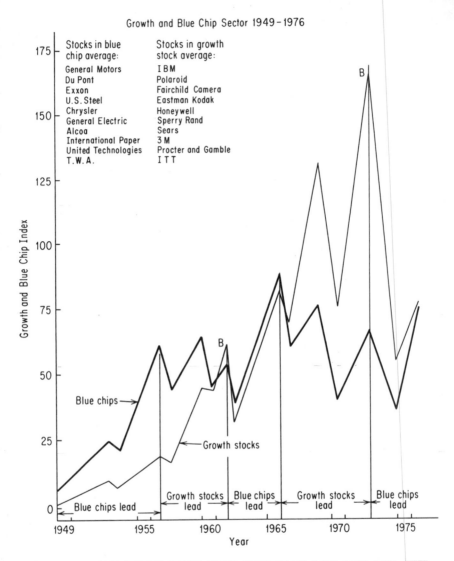

Growth and Blue Chip Sector 1949–1976

Stocks in blue chip average:
General Motors
Du Pont
Exxon
U.S. Steel
Chrysler
General Electric
Alcoa
International Paper
United Technologies
T.W.A.

Stocks in growth stock average:
I B M
Polaroid
Fairchild Camera
Eastman Kodak
Honeywell
Sperry Rand
Sears
3 M
Procter and Gamble
I T T

CHART 7 FOLLOWING THEIR MILD BREAKS IN 1957 AND 1966, THE GROWTH SECTOR WAS READY TO DOMINATE THE MARKET THROUGH TWO STAGES. After their second stage of leadership (pt. B) (1960–61; 70–72)—which was also the last stage of a broad bull market—these stocks experienced a sharp break (1962, 1973–74). During the following period, the blue chips led until about one year after the DJIA made a new all-time high.

growth[2] and the blue chip sector, depending upon how we perceive risk.

The blue chips emerge from their depressed levels and participate rather fully in the first broad bull market of the expansionary phase of the cycle. Among the leaders during this time are those industries and companies which had become dominant during the last economic cycle. This leadership results from the fact that the dominant industry spans two cycles, emerging in the latter part of one and extending its dominance into the early part of the next cycle. The railroad industry started to become dominant around 1850. In the 10 years to 1906, the beginning of the following cycle, the Dow Jones Rail Average increased 333%. Similarly, the automobile industry began its dominance around 1910; and from 1949 to 1959, the beginning of the present cycle, the price of General Motors, the leading car manufacturer, increased over 600%.

During this first broad bull market, most of the blue chips become fully recognized—future earnings growth is adequately or more than adequately discounted. After this time, the dynamic moves within the blue chip sector occur when a depressed industry or company, by solving its problems, returns to investor favor. This change in stock leadership has to do with the shifting fundamentals of various industries. In good times, some of the older industries become plagued with competition, excess capacity, or other problems which lead to long periods wherein the industry sells at depressed levels. This occurrence can be seen in the stock market when during the first or second stage of a bull market, the stock prices of an industry group break the low established in a previous decline; for example, the low made during 1957 was broken during the 1960 stock market break (see Chart 8). This inability to stay above a prior low during the course of a broad bull market means that

---

[2]The other segment of the speculative sector, low-priced stocks, may also participate at the same time that investors favor growth stocks. By blossoming forth with a new product or an innovative technique, a low-priced stock within one of the older industries may threaten to increase its importance or its place within the industry and thus experience a dramatic increase in price. This was the case with American Motors in 1959 and Natomas in 1969.

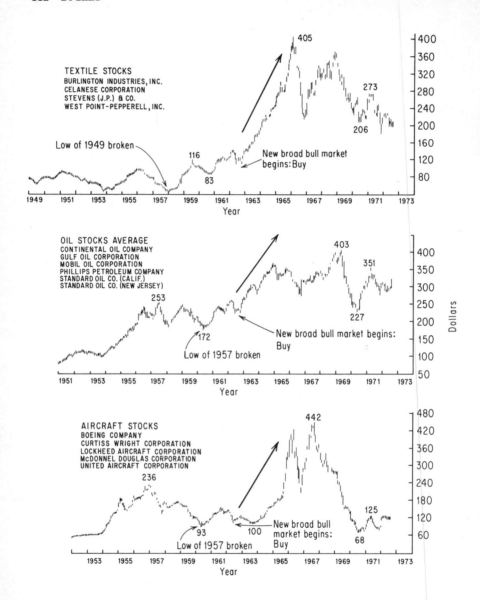

TEXTILE STOCKS
BURLINGTON INDUSTRIES, INC.
CELANESE CORPORATION
STEVENS (J.P.) & CO.
WEST POINT-PEPPERELL, INC.

Low of 1949 broken

116

83

New broad bull market
begins: Buy

405

273

206

OIL STOCKS AVERAGE
CONTINENTAL OIL COMPANY
GULF OIL CORPORATION
MOBIL OIL CORPORATION
PHILLIPS PETROLEUM COMPANY
STANDARD OIL CO. (CALIF.)
STANDARD OIL CO. (NEW JERSEY)

253

172

Low of 1957 broken

New broad bull market begins:
Buy

403

351

227

Dollars

AIRCRAFT STOCKS
BOEING COMPANY
CURTISS WRIGHT CORPORATION
LOCKHEED AIRCRAFT CORPORATION
McDONNEL DOUGLAS CORPORATION
UNITED AIRCRAFT CORPORATION

236

93

Low of 1957 broken

100

New broad bull
market begins:
Buy

442

68

125

Adapted from M.C. HORSEY & CO, The Stock Picture

**CHART 8   TEXTILES, OILS, AIRCRAFT 1952–1971. These groups performed poorly
during the 1950s. During the course of the broad bull market the low price made
during a preceding stage was broken. And, during the next period, they outperformed
the market.**

investors have recognized the poor prospects of this industry and have turned pessimistic.

Yet, these depressed stock levels motivate management to tackle its problems. Capital spending is deferred, unprofitable lines are dropped, and inefficient workers are fired. At the same time, owing to price cuts or discounts, the market for the product of these industries expands. As excess capacity is worked off and demand increases, these industries become more profitable. During the initial stage of the next broad bull market, they usually become the leaders. During the broad bull market that began in 1962, it was those industries—the oils, textiles, and aircrafts, which had sold at depressed levels during the latter part of the previous era—that led the way among the blue chips.

For example, in 1960, the price for the oil industry group took out its 1957 low (see Chart 8). This industry had suffered from a glut of cheap foreign oil which depressed domestic oil prices. However, during this time, new markets, such as petrochemicals, were springing up, and efforts were being made to restrict cheap imports. A mandatory quota on imports was instituted and the oil industry soon prospered. In the early part of the following broad bull market, these stocks were among the leaders.[3]

The same holds true for individual companies within the blue chip sector. However, in the case of individual stocks, it was those companies which made a 12-year low following the first or second stage of a bull market[4]—that is, during the break of 1957 or 1960 in the broad bull market that began in 1949—that qualified as having sold at depressed levels. As 12 years has been about the average length of a market cycle from the bottom of a broad bull market to the bottom of the following broad bull market, these companies, unlike most others, are selling below their price at roughly the comparable stage in the prior broad bull market. Amidst this background of investor pessimism, management takes aggressive measures to

---

[3]The steels, chemicals, and papers which had sold at depressed levels during the 1960s and early 1970s were among the leaders in the broad bull market which began in 1974. (See Chart 10.)

[4]The break following the third stage does not qualify, as there is not enough time for revitalization prior to the beginning of the next broad bull market.

improve the company's position. In the first part of the following broad bull market, these companies typically outperform the market. Of the 255 stocks in the Horsey stock book,[5] 22 qualified as having made a 12-year low during the broad bull market of 1949–1961 (see Table 8-1 and Chart 9). In the following broad bull market, most of these companies experienced a significant change for the better— usually before their reported earnings showed a considerable improvement—and outperformed the market. From their June 1962 low to their 1967–1969 high, these companies appreciated an average of 565%. By 1969, 18 of these 22 stocks had at least tripled in

---

[5]M. C. Horsey & Co., "The 25-Year Picture," Salisbury, Maryland, October, 1969.

TABLE 8-1   BROAD BULL MARKET OF 1949–1961: STOCKS THAT MADE A 12-YEAR LOW*

	Low, June 1962	High, 1964–1966	High, 1967–1969	% gain to 1967–1969	Low, 1970–1971	Earnings	
						1961	1968–1969, whichever is higher
Atlas	2	4½	8	300	3	(.21)[‡]	.07
Bucyrus Erie	4½	26	31	600	15	.37	2.10
Burlington	10	50	51	400	28	.92	3.10
Case	5	32	26	400	†	(11.74)	.22
Celanese	30	92	76	150	50	2.11	5.41
Chadburn	5½	8	20	300	3	.51	.84
Chrysler	10	61	72	600	16	.31	6.23
Coca Cola	18	45	88	400	63	.77	2.20
Commercial Solvent	16	79	57	250	16	1.90	.68
General Host	6	22	45	600	7	(.77)	1.34
Kresge	4½	15	60	1300	34	.27	1.56
Lake Shore Mines	3	4	9½	200	2½	.31	.07
McCrory	18	25	37	100	14	.72	2.84
Penn Central	10	73	86	750	4	.94	3.91
St. Joe Lead	8	26	39	400	20	.71	4.37
Swift	16½	32	36	125	22	1.00	1.63
Texas Gulf Sulphur	4	43	53	1200	12	.42	2.33
TWA	8	100	90	1000	10	(2.21)	1.97
U.S. Smelting	6	80	79	1200	20	.15	4.38
USM	24	35	52	100	11	1.77	3.62
Woolworth	21	33	43	100	26	1.59	2.32
White Consolidated	2	22	42	2000	8	(.23)	2.65
				Average 565%			

*Also, American Motors, Gulf & Western, Technicolor, and Studebaker Worthington made 12-year lows during this broad bull market, but as these stocks had subsequent price increases of more than 500% prior to the following broad bull market, it was likely that they had already experienced their significant advance.

†Acquired by Tenneco.

‡Parentheses indicate deficit.

price, with 9 of the 18 showing an increase of more than 500%. And 17 of the 52 stocks that qualified as having made a 12-year low during the broad bull market of 1962–1973[6] had, by August 1977, tripled in price from their December 1974 low (see Table 8-2).

Just as the depressed blue chips of one broad bull market are likely to solve their problems and become the leaders in the next, the leading blue chips of one broad bull market are likely to develop problems and become the laggards during the next bull market. The reason is that these industries do not have an unlimited ability to increase the scope of their market—they have already reached maturity. Just as a long period of economic prosperity leads us to overdo things in the economy, so a period of heightened stock prices and earnings leads to new companies entering the industry and older companies increasing their capacity. In addition, management becomes less concerned about costs and allows a considerable amount of fat to occur; labor demands and gets higher wages; and marginally profitable projects are undertaken in the hope that their markets will strengthen eventually. At the same time, markets are lost as aggressive pricing leads users to seek substitutes. The aluminums, steels, and papers which led the way during the 1950s were in general the laggards during the next broad bull market (see Chart 11).

During the 1950s, the steel companies experienced a remarkable period of prosperity. Yet, while they were doing so, capacity mounted as foreign countries attempted to become self-sufficient in steel (in a period of a few years the United States went from being a net exporter to being a large importer of steel), and costs rose, as labor was able to extract increased wages. At the same time, steel users were stressing greater economy in steel usage (using lighter weights and reducing the level of their inventories) and turning to substitutes (such as prestressed concrete and plastics). During the following intermediate cycle, steel became a sick industry and could not participate in the accompanying broad bull market. This case shows what happens in the blue chip sector: As an industry increases its control over the environment, it is likely to prosper, and

---

[6]In this case, "The 25-Year Picture," published by M. C. Horsey & Co., October, 1972, was used.

CHRYSLER CORPORATION

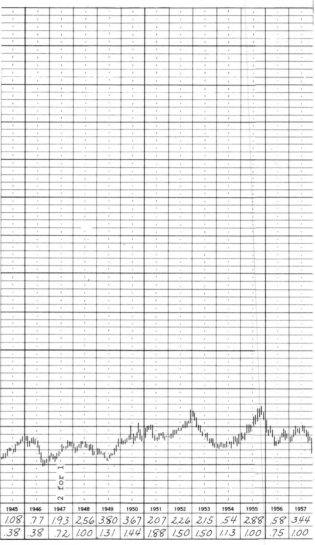

	1945	1946	1947	1948	1949	1950	1951	1952	1953	1954	1955	1956	1957
	1.08	.77	1.93	2.56	3.80	3.67	2.07	2.26	2.15	.54	2.88	.58	3.44
	.38	.38	.72	1.00	1.31	1.44	1.88	1.50	1.50	1.13	1.00	.75	1.00

COURTESY OF

M. C. HORSEY & COMPANY, Publishers, 120 South Blvd., SALISBURY, MD. 21801

CHART 9 *a* **CHRYSLER, PENN CENTRAL, T.W.A. These are three of the companies that sold at depressed levels during the broad bull market which extended from 1949 to 1961. And during the next broad bull market, these stocks outperformed the market.**

Chrysler, Imperial, Dodge, Plymouth & Valiant Cars, Dodge & Fargo Trucks - Also Automotive Parts,
Heating & Air Conditioning Equip't, Marine & Industrial Engines, Defense-Space Products, etc.

600% increase

New broad bull market begins
Buy

Split 2 for 1
Split 2 for 1

12 year low

1970 low
16-1/8

	1958	1959	1960	1961	1962	1963	1964	1965	1966	1967	1968	1969	1970	1971	1972	YEAR
EARN.	d.97	d.16	.90	.31	1.81	4.35	5.50	5.44	4.16	4.35	6.23					
DIV.	.38	.25	.38	.25	.25	.44	*1.00	1.25	2.00	2.00	2.00					

PENN CENTRAL COMPANY

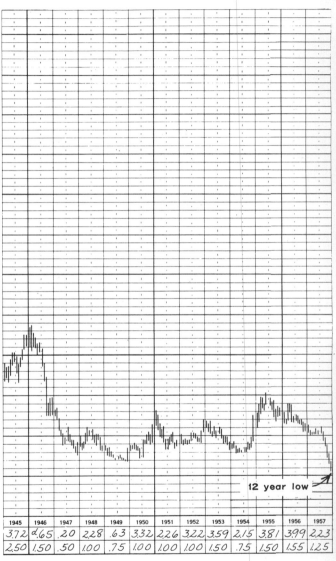

	1945	1946	1947	1948	1949	1950	1951	1952	1953	1954	1955	1956	1957
	3.72	d.65	.20	2.28	.63	3.32	2.26	3.22	3.59	2.15	3.81	3.99	2.23
	2.50	1.50	.50	1.00	.75	1.00	1.00	1.00	1.50	.75	1.50	1.55	1.25

12 year low

COURTESY OF
M. C. HORSEY & COMPANY, Publishers, 120 South Blvd., SALISBURY, MD. 21801

CHART 9b

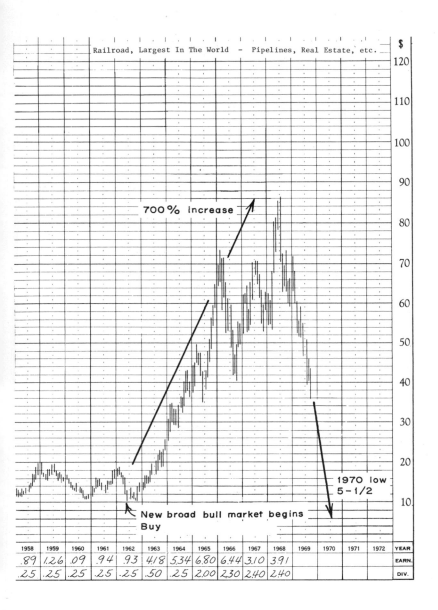

Railroad, Largest In The World - Pipelines, Real Estate, etc.

700% increase

New broad bull market begins
Buy

1970 low
5-1/2

YEAR	1958	1959	1960	1961	1962	1963	1964	1965	1966	1967	1968	1969	1970	1971	1972
EARN.	.89	1.26	.09	.94	.93	4.18	5.34	6.80	6.44	3.10	3.91				
DIV.	.25	.25	.25	.25	.25	.50	.25	2.00	2.30	2.40	2.40				

TRANS WORLD AIR LINES, INC.

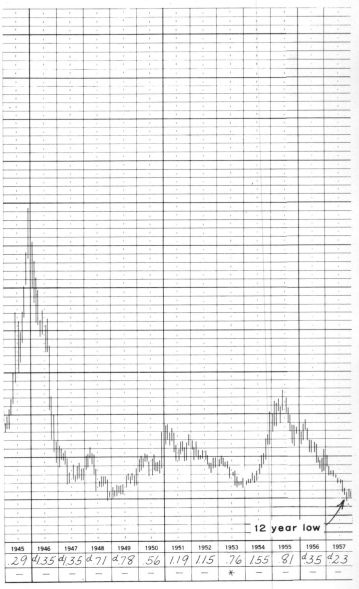

	1945	1946	1947	1948	1949	1950	1951	1952	1953	1954	1955	1956	1957
	.29	d1.35	d1.35	d.71	d.78	.56	1.19	1.15	.76	1.55	.81	d.35	d.23
	—	—	—	—	—	—	—	—	*	—	—	—	—

12 year low

COURTESY OF
M. C. HORSEY & COMPANY, Publishers, 120 South Blvd., SALISBURY, MD. 21801

CHART 9c

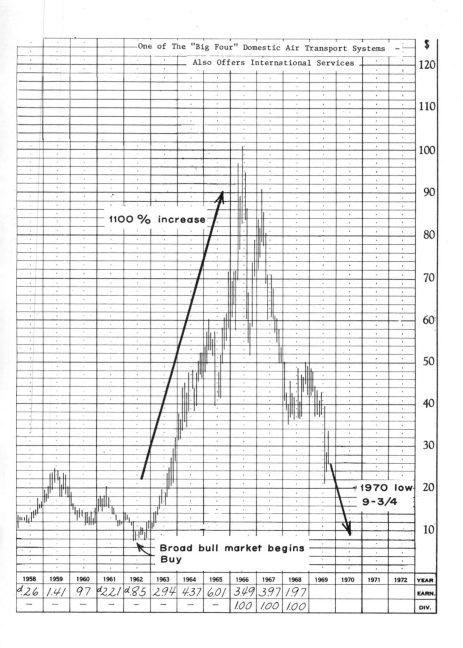

One of The "Big Four" Domestic Air Transport Systems — Also Offers International Services

1100 % increase

Broad bull market begins
Buy

1970 low
9-3/4

YEAR	1958	1959	1960	1961	1962	1963	1964	1965	1966	1967	1968	1969	1970	1971	1972
EARN.	d.26	1.41	.97	d2.21	d.85	2.94	4.37	6.01	3.49	3.97	1.97				
DIV.	—	—	—	—	—	—	—	—	1.00	1.00	1.00				

TABLE 8-2   BROAD BULL MARKET OF 1962–1973: STOCKS THAT MADE A 12-YEAR LOW*

	Low, December 1974	High, 1976– August 1977	Earnings 1973
Addressograph-Multigraph	4	15†	.40
Airco	10	34†	1.66
Alcan	19	30	2.42
Allied Chemical	27	51	3.45
Allis Chalmers	7	33†	1.30
Alcoa	26	61	3.09
American Can	25	41	3.58
American Motors	3½	5½	1.65
Armco Steel	21	35	3.38
Babcock Wilcox	12	48†	1.82
Bendix	15	47†	3.14
Bethlehem Steel	24	48	4.72
Budd	7	23†	3.60
Burlington Northern	33	53	4.01
Columbia Pictures	2	16†	(6.45)‡
Consolidated Edison	6½	25†	2.34
Crown Zellerbach	20	49	4.28
Detroit Edison	7½	18	1.77
Du Pont	85	161	12.04
El Paso Natural Gas	10	20	2.05
Ex-Cell-o	9½	29†	2.07
GAF	6½	17	1.85
General Dynamics	16	64†	3.84
Great A&P	7	15	.49
INA Corp.	26	48	4.71
Libby Owens Ford	12½	37½†	5.15
Liggett & Meyers	24	35	3.39

*International Minerals & Chemicals also made a 12-year low during this broad bull market, but had a subsequent increase of more than 500% prior to the following broad bull market. And Marcor was acquired by Mobil.

its prosperity is likely to lead to its losing control over the environment.

The return to prosperity or heightened industry importance may require some conceptualization that problems are being solved, for, by the time conclusive evidence is available, the market is likely

	Low, December 1974	High, 1976– August 1977	Earnings 1973
Lockheed	4	19†	1.20
Martin Marietta	13	29	2.59
May	13	36	2.10
Mead	8	24†	1.77
Molycorp	14	59†	2.46
Monsanto	40	100	6.90
NCR	13	46†	3.00
National Gypsum	8	18	1.93
Norfolk & Western	19	37	2.18
NL	12	24	1.95
PPG	22	59	4.48
Philadelphia Electric	9½	21	1.99
Republic Steel	22	40	5.36
Reynolds Metal	14	44†	1.80
Rockwell Industries	19	37	4.08
Scott Paper	12	24	1.63
Santa Fe Industries	26	42	4.01
Sherwin Williams	32	43	4.36
Signal	13	34	2.33
Standard Oil of California	21	45	4.97
Twentieth Century Fox	4½	25†	.90
Union Carbide	37	77	4.78
U.S. Gypsum	13	27	2.90
U.S. Steel	24	59	4.01
White Motors	8	8	2.46

Average appreciation 167%

†Tripled in price from their December 1974 lows.
‡Parentheses indicate deficit.

already to be well on its way to discounting the companies' improvement.

The best time to buy the stocks that made a 12-year low following the first or second stage of a broad bull market is usually at the beginning of the following broad bull market. As they are discount-

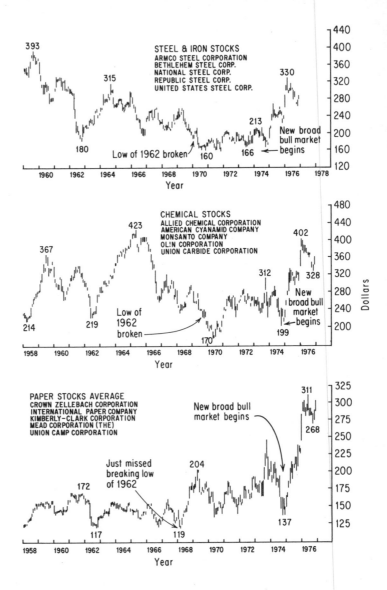

Adapted from M.C. HORSEY & CO , The Stock Picture

CHART 10   STEELS, CHEMICALS, PAPERS. These groups performed poorly during the last broad bull market (1962–73) and during the first stage of the current broad bull market they appear to have been the leaders.

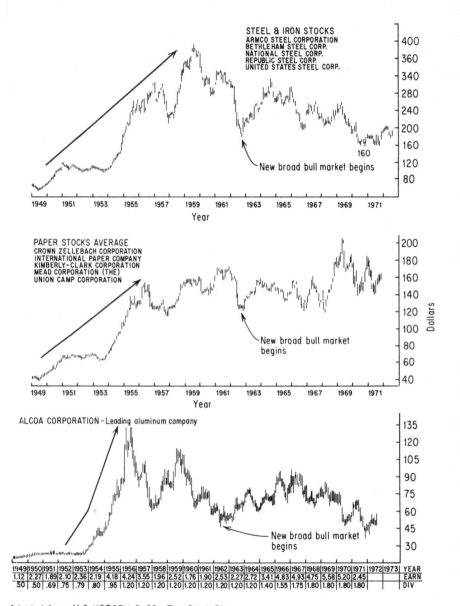

STEEL & IRON STOCKS
ARMCO STEEL CORPORATION
BETHLEHAM STEEL CORP.
NATIONAL STEEL CORP.
REPUBLIC STEEL CORP.
UNITED STATES STEEL CORP.

New broad bull market begins

160

PAPER STOCKS AVERAGE
CROWN ZELLEBACH CORPORATION
INTERNATIONAL PAPER COMPANY
KIMBERLY-CLARK CORPORATION
MEAD CORPORATION (THE)
UNION CAMP CORPORATION

New broad bull market begins

Dollars

ALCOA CORPORATION - Leading aluminum company

New broad bull market begins

Year

YEAR	1949	1950	1951	1952	1953	1954	1955	1956	1957	1958	1959	1960	1961	1962	1963	1964	1965	1966	1967	1968	1969	1970	1971	1972	1973
EARN	1.12	2.27	1.89	2.10	2.36	2.19	4.18	4.24	3.55	1.96	2.52	1.76	1.90	2.53	2.27	2.72	3.41	4.83	4.93	4.75	5.58	5.20	2.45		
DIV	.50	.50	.69	.75	.79	.80	.95	1.20	1.20	1.20	1.20	1.20	1.20	1.20	1.20	1.20	1.40	1.55	1.75	1.80	1.80	1.80	1.80		

Adapted from M.C. HORSEY & CO, The Stock Picture

**CHART 11 STEELS, PAPERS, ALUMINUMS. Following their outstanding per-
formance of the early 1950s, these stocks were unable to participate in the broad
bull market of the 1960s.**

ing the worst, the risk of owning these depressed stocks is quite low at these times. And the earnings improvements which usually follow thus have a significant impact on share prices.

However, while these stocks are among the leaders of a broad bull market, by the second stage of this bull market they usually begin a long period of underperforming the market—often at the very time that Wall Street is becoming favorable to them. By 1970, during the break in the stock market following the second stage, 14 of these stocks had lost 50%—9 of them as much as 75%—of their former value. Thus, it is important to recognize that while these stocks may be vehicles to take advantage of the early part of a broad bull market, they are not stocks to fall in love with.

In the growth sector, the most exciting companies are those of the new, innovative industry, along with its supporting companies and related cousins. This is so because the market of such industries continues to expand along with the growth of the industry. The increased sales of autos led to the building of more roads and the dispersion of people and industry, which, in turn, led to a demand for more autos. On the other hand, a series of marginal or faddish types of industries (bowling, nursing homes, fast foods, franchising) flourish briefly and then fall from grace, producing for their holders more disappointments than profits. As their markets do not expand, usually these marginal industries cannot survive the competition and overcrowding that develops during their periods of prosperity. To find those industries which have expanding markets, it is necessary to assess the changes occurring within our economic system and understand the meaning of new processes and schemes.

Throughout our whole industrial revolution we kept coming up with new sources of energy and power, from steam and coal to oil to electricity, to provide an innovative process by which humans made giant strides in their ability to cope with the natural world. The four innovations—cotton, railroads, autos, and computers—that dominated our supercycles followed in a natural evolutionary pattern. Each of these innovations, by providing either a new material, a new form of transportation, or new methods of information gathering, added a new dimension to our handling of the material world. There were materials before cotton, transportation before the railroad, and the computer was preceded by the telegraph and newsprint; however, these older techniques failed to enable us to take an enormous forward leap in our ability to control and master nature.

Each innovation promised people an increased ability to cope with life, and in so doing, provided a tremendous psychological lift. Cotton and autos provided ordinary persons with a heretofore-denied means to enhance their appearance or become mobile. Railroads and computers allowed business to build on the benefits of mass organization and thus to expand its markets.

In each case, we came to see ourselves as more powerful and to change the way we did things. A restructuring of our economic system took place. We became dependent upon these new industries. Just as meatpacking was dependent on the railroads, or the building of suburbia on cars, so banking, finance, and medicine are today becoming dependent on computers. Yet, in order to make great economic strides, each innovative form—for example, a new form of transportation—first had to serve business before the technique could provide a product for mass consumption. Therefore, it was necessary for the railroad to precede the auto and for the computer to come before any innovation involving mass communication.

By solving an economic problem, we become ready to take on new dimensions. New materials and forms of transportation, such as those which came after cotton and the auto—steel, chemicals, airplanes, and the spaceship, no longer become new key industries. They now play a supporting role to other innovations, helping us further to refine the efficiency of conducting our business.

During the 1860s and 1870s it appeared—especially in Germany—that chemicals might be the new dominant industry. However, chemicals were out of tune with what was happening in our industrial revolution. The big innovation at this time was the development of new forms of transportation. And the next step after the railroad was a form of transportation that could serve the individual directly—the auto. In addition, chemicals were not the result of a new source of energy and were therefore unlikely to spawn the technology for related technological developments.

In the late 1920s, the wave of the future to far-seeing investors appeared to be the radio. While these investors did grasp that the next step in the industrial revolution would be the use of electricity to help further our ability to gather and use information, they failed to recognize that business had to be served first. So, rather than RCA and the radio, it was IBM and the computer which became the key innovative industry of the next cycle.

Each new key industry provided the cycle with its growth, spawned related industries, and provided the romance around which the business legends were woven. During England's first cycle, it was the stories of those who made their fortunes in cotton— Robert Owen, Richard Arkwright, James Watt, etc.—that were continuously being retold. Shipping came to play an important part, for it was the transportation that was used to bring cotton home to Britain and carry finished products to foreign markets. In the following cycle, the stories that dealt with laying the tracks of the Southern Pacific—or with the intrigues (involving Cornelius Vanderbilt, Jay Gould, Daniel Drew, and Jim Fisk) relating to the Erie Railroad— provided our romance. Iron, steel, and coal came to assume places of importance, for they served as the material or fuel of the railroads. In the next cycle, we got the auto, the story of Henry Ford, and the building of General Motors. Rubber and oil, by serving as automotive material and fuel, became important. Currently, we meet with the computer and our glamour company, IBM. The knowledge revolution, in once again leading to a restructuring of our business life, is fashioning the same giant steps forward that railroads and autos did previously. And the semiconductor and electronic industries are providing the necessary parts and equipment to support the theme of this new revolution.

Once we identify these key industries, our remaining task is finding those companies that are in a position to enter a claim or challenge for industry leadership. Those companies that are putting in a bid for a place of industry leadership—that is, to be among the top three companies—provide most of the opportunities among the growth stocks. In the 1860s and 1870s, such fights occurred among the railroads. During the 1920s, we saw General Motors overtake Ford as the leading auto company. And soon afterward, Chrysler and Studebaker made sustained bids for leading roles in that industry. In our present cycle, we saw IBM surpass Sperry Rand, the developer of Univac. And important bids for leadership roles were recently put in by Control Data, Burroughs, Sperry Rand, etc. In the play for leadership in our supporting industries, we see the fight between Fairchild Camera, Motorola, and Texas Instruments in semiconductors. In providing a miniaturized memory device, semiconductors have become the basic building blocks for computers and other high technology products. In the supporting side of our knowledge industry, copying and data communications, we saw first the rise of Apeco (in the early 1960s) and then its being overtaken by Xerox. And in the television segment of the mass communications industry, we witnessed the growth of RCA and Zenith.

Once we recognize that some company is putting in a bid for industry leadership, e.g., Burroughs's bid for the number two spot in computers during the late 1960s and early 1970s, the best time to buy into this company is usually either one year after the Dow makes new all-time highs or during the break that follows the first stage of a broad bull market, whichever comes first (see Chart 12). By this time, the company has begun its period of superior market performance, which usually lasts until the end of the broad bull market.

The outlook for an individual stock depends upon the sector to which it belongs. Following a serious contraction, the blue chip stocks usually have a significant rise—especially those stocks which have experienced a broad bear market. However, as earnings growth is rather quickly recognized as unsustainable, these stocks only participate for short periods.

On the other hand, the growth stocks are likely to participate for long periods during the expansionary phase of our cycle. They tend to get recurring broad bull markets that correspond to the intermediate cycles of the expansionary phase. Then, in the latter stages of their bull market, after the blue chips have suffered considerable damage (or about one year after the DJIA makes a new all-time high), they usually dominate the market. In this case, the assumption is that this earnings growth will be sustainable for a long period of time. The meaning of earnings growth differs, however, depending upon the sector the stock belongs to.

As we entered the third intermediate cycle of our current expansionary phase, we found the basic industry stocks—steels, aluminums, papers, chemicals—leading the way, while the growths were lagging. This is as it should be. However, once the second stage of this broad bull market begins the growth stocks, with IBM and those

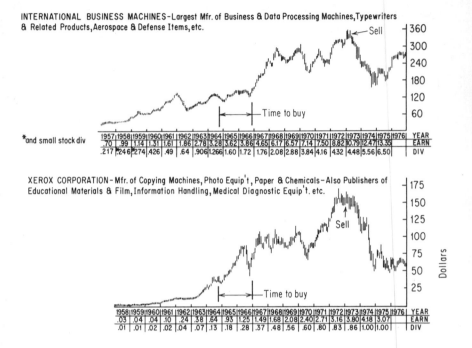

INTERNATIONAL BUSINESS MACHINES–Largest Mfr. of Business & Data Processing Machines,Typewriters & Related Products,Aerospace & Defense Items,etc.

Sell

Time to buy

360
300
240
180
120
60

*and small stock div

YEAR	1957	1958	1959	1960	1961	1962	1963	1964	1965	1966	1967	1968	1969	1970	1971	1972	1973	1974	1975	1976
EARN	.70	.99	1.14	1.31	1.61	1.86	2.78	3.28	3.62	3.86	4.65	6.17	6.57	7.14	7.50	8.82	10.79	12.47	13.35	
DIV	.217	.246	.274	.426	.49	.64	.906	1.266	1.60	1.72	1.76	2.08	2.88	3.84	4.16	4.32	4.48	5.56	6.50	

XEROX CORPORATION–Mfr. of Copying Machines, Photo Equip't, Paper & Chemicals–Also Publishers of Educational Materials & Film,Information Handling, Medical Diagnostic Equip't. etc.

175
150
125
100
75
50
25

Sell

Time to buy

Dollars

YEAR	1958	1959	1960	1961	1962	1963	1964	1965	1966	1967	1968	1969	1970	1971	1972	1973	1974	1975	1976
EARN	.03	.04	.04	.10	.24	.38	.64	.93	1.25	1.49	1.68	2.08	2.40	2.71	3.16	3.80	4.18	3.07	
DIV	.01	.01	.02	.02	.04	.07	.13	.18	.28	.37	.48	.56	.60	.80	.83	.86	1.00	1.00	

TEXAS INSTRUMENTS, INC.– Mfr. of Semiconductor Devices, Electronic Components & Equipment, etc.

Sell

Time to buy

140
120
100
80
60
40
20

YEAR	1958	1959	1960	1961	1962	1963	1964	1965	1966	1967	1968	1969	1970	1971	1972	1973	1974	1975	1976
EARN	.37	.72	.78	.47	.43	.60	.90	1.23	1.65	1.06	1.20	1.53	1.36	1.52	2.17	3.67	3.92	2.71	
DIV	–	–	–	–	.12	.16	.20	.25	.28	.38	.40	.40	.40	.40	.42	.56	.92	1.00	

Adapted from M.C. HORSEY & CO , The Stock Picture

CHART 12 IBM, XEROX, TEXAS INSTRUMENTS, SPERRY RAND, AND MOTOROLA, 1958–1976. The growth stocks were outstanding buys from about one year after the Dow made a new all-time high through the break following the first stage of the broad bull market. In the following eight years, they appreciated anywhere from 250 to 600 %. On the other hand, each of these stocks broke 50 % or more from its high following the third stage of the 1962–1973 broad bull market. The 1974 shakeout in the growth stocks has again provided an opportunity to consider these stocks at reasonable prices and following the first stage of this broad bull market, these stocks should put in an outstanding performance once again.

SPERRY RAND CORPORATION – Mfr. of Aviation & Marine Navigation Instruments, Pumps, Valves, etc. Also Office Equipment, Business Machines, "Univac", etc.

	1956	1957	1958	1959	1960	1961	1962	1963	1964	1965	1966	1967	1968	1969	1970	1971	1972	1973	1974	1975	1976	YEAR
	1.74	.96	.96	1.30	.95	.81	.43	.85	.70	1.02	1.73	1.94	2.26	2.37	2.11	1.77	2.62	3.27	3.81	4.19		EARN
	.80	.80	.80	.80	.80	*	*	–	–	–	–	.10	.40	.48	.50	.55	.60	.63	.71	.76		DIV

MOTOROLA, INC. – Mfr. Radios, Semiconductors, Communications Equipment, etc.

	1957	1958	1959	1960	1961	1962	1963	1964	1965	1966	1967	1968	1969	1970	1971	1972	1973	1974	1975	1976	YEAR
	.34	.32	.60	.53	.40	.55	.54	.86	1.31	1.35	.77	1.15	1.37	.96	1.18	1.91	2.95	2.52	1.46		EARN
	.13	.13	.13	.15	.17	.17	.17	.17	.25	.25	.25	.25	.25	.28	.30	.31	.40	.55	.70		DIV

Adapted from M.C. HORSEY & CO, The Stock Picture

companies concentrating on making smaller computers among them, are likely again to move to the front. For the innovative industries typically experience a surge of growth during the third intermediate cycle of an expansionary phase.

Let us now turn our attention to another speculative medium—commodities.

NINE

COMMODITY CYCLES

During each cyclical expansion we typically get two huge inflations which generally accompany or follow a war. During the last (what appears to be a 54-year) economic cycle, these inflations accompanied the Spanish-American War and World War I, and in the present cycle they followed World War II and Vietnam. The dramatic up moves in commodity prices occurred at these times, with two important exceptions—the great bull market in rubber following the introduction of the automobile during the early 1900s, and the 1962–1963 sugar bull market which followed Castro's takeover of Cuba. As a result of the ensuing trade war, the United States was forced into the free sugar market (where only about 15% of the sugar produced is traded) in order to fill its needs. During these inflations, commodities offer a viable alternative to stocks (see Chart 13).

Not all commodities present the same opportunity, however. The reason is that each commodity has its own pattern of recurring broad bull or broad bear markets, depending upon whether the long-term demand for the commodity is growing or not. Those commodities for which demand is increasing get recurring broad bull markets that usually extend through two stages. This is so because, following a sharp falloff in prices, supplies are cut too much in face of a growing demand. It then takes two stages before supplies again outpace demand.

However, those commodities, where demand is diminishing, get recurring broad bear markets that also usually extend through two

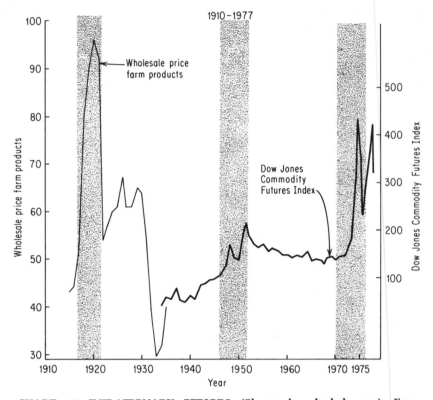

CHART 13 INFLATIONARY PERIODS (Shown by shaded area). From 1914 to 1933, the wholesale price farm product index; from 1933 until 1977, Dow Jones Commodity Futures Index.

stages. The reason is that, following a sharp rise in prices, supplies are built up too much in face of a diminishing demand. It then takes two stages to work off the resulting overburdensome supplies.

Each particular supply-and-demand situation[1] (such as the 1963–1964 soybean situation or the 1966 egg situation) is part of these broader bull or bear markets. We can see this pattern by looking at soybeans and eggs.

The Soybean Market Soybeans have witnessed a phenomenal growth in consumption from 235 million bushels in 1949–1950 to

---

[1]The period of producing and distributing one crop; this is the time frame that we usually deal with in commodities.

1485 million bushels in the 1975–1976 crop year. The bulk of these soybeans is either exported or else processed (crushed) into soybean oil and soybean meal. Soybean oil is used mostly as an edible vegetable oil and soybean meal is a high protein animal feed, with the biggest proportion going to hogs. Each crop year begins on September 1 when harvesting of beans planted in late spring commences and extends through the following August.

Soybeans, because they are a commodity with a growing demand, experience recurring broad bull markets. Each broad bull market lasts until we experience a buildup in supplies which far exceeds demand. This surplus results in a sharp break in prices which restimulates demand and thus sets off another long, two-staged bull market.

Let us look at the five-year period beginning in the fall of 1961 and extending until the fall of 1966 (Chart 14). The 1961–1962 crop year followed the big price advance of 1961, wherein prices increased from a monthly average of $2.11 per bushel in November 1960 to a monthly average of $3.20 per bushel in the following April. Production, which was encouraged by these higher prices and an increase in the government's support price (the price at which farmers can dispose of their crops to the government) from $2.05 to $2.50, expanded to 693 million bushels, which was 21% more than usage during the 1960–1961 crop year. (See Table 9-1.) At that time, owing to the same higher prices, the sharp long-term uptrend in soybean usage had come to a halt. From mid-September to December of 1961, consumption increased by less than 3% from the year before, the smallest increase since the fall of 1951 (see Table 9-1, column 5). This three-and-a-half-month period at the beginning of a crop year provides a good indication of how usage is faring in relation to the prior year. By projecting this figure we can get indicated demand for the current crop year (Table 9-1, column 6). This huge increase in production relative to indicated usage (18% more) resulted in a fall in the monthly average price of soybeans to $2.45 per bushel, along with an increase in the carry-over to 58 million bushels—a three-year high—by September 1962, the end of the crop year.

Yet, just as a serious contraction sets the stage for a long period of sustained economic growth, an increase in soybean production by 8% or more over indicated usage has in the past usually led to a broad bull market (see Table 9-1). The resulting large price decline,

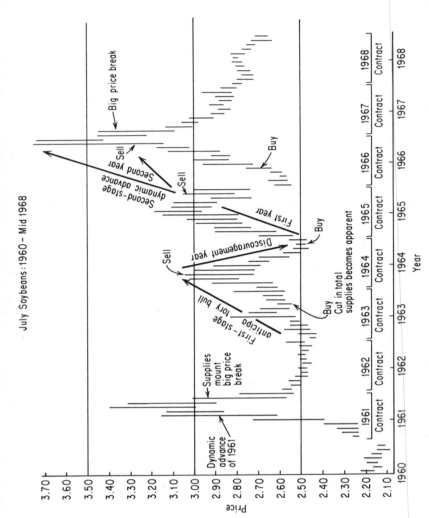

CHART 14 MONTHLY CHART.

together with a cut in the price support as the government (usually) becomes worried about a further buildup in soybean supplies, discourages further vast increases in production as many soybean producers switch to corn or cotton.[2] As a consequence, the resumption of the sharp long-term uptrend in usage occurs against a more modest buildup in supplies.

In the 1962–1963 crop year, production fell to 675 million bushels, just 7½% more than the previous year's consumption. But, from mid-September to December of 1962, usage was 13% higher than in the previous year. At this rate of usage, the carry-over at the end of this crop year would be reduced to 25 million bushels.[3] Indeed, when planting intentions were released in March of 1963 and showed an increase of only 4%, it became apparent that the buildup in total supplies had ended. Given average yields, which indicated a production increase of only 27 million bushels, total supplies for the following crop year would be 6 million bushels less than in the current year.[4]

This recognition of the first cut in total soybean supplies set off the first stage in a broad bull market in soybeans. Many people, remembering the price advance that had occurred in 1961, the last time supplies had become scarce, bought beans in anticipation of another such supply shortage. This advance can be called the anticipatory stage because people are beginning to take a position and prices rise *before supplies are actually scarce*. The November soybean contract advanced from $2.45 in mid-April 1963 to $2.91½ early in November.[5]

However, by the beginning of the 1963–1964 crop year this anticipatory price advance had reached a level which restrained demand.

---

[2]Many farmers are able to produce both soybeans and either corn or cotton, and shift their production to take advantage of the prospective prices of these competing crops.

[3]As the most important demand factor, a larger spring pig crop in 1963—which meant an increase in demand for soybean meal—had yet to be felt, this estimate was fairly conservative.

[4]The cut in total supplies actually came to 13 million bushels.

[5]As we can see in Table 9-2, had we bought one contract of November soybeans on April 15 at $2.45⅜ and sold on November 8, 1963, at $2.88¼, we would have made $2175. And we never would have been subjected to a paper loss of more than ¼¢, or $12.50 per contract.

TABLE 9-1 SOYBEAN STATISTICS (in millions of bushels)

Crop year	Beginning carry-over (1)	Production[1] (2)	Total supplies[1] (3)	Consumption (4)
(beginning Oct. 1)				
1949–50	3.2	227	230	235
RA 1950–51	2.9	287	290	298
1951–52[4]	4.2	281	285	284
1952–53[5]	3.6	292	296	292
1953–54[6]	10.1	262	272	278
1954–55	1.3	343	344	333
1955–56	9.9	371	381	380
1956–57	3.7	456	460	443
RA 1957–58	9.9	480	490	472
1958–59[4]	21.1	574	595	539
1959–60[5]	62.1	538	600	572
1960–61[6]	23.2	559	582	573
RA 1961–62	6.0	693	699	628
1962–63[4]	57.6	675	733	712
1963–64[5]	15.1	702	717	682
1964–65[6]	32.0	700	732	724
Crop year changed from Oct. 1st to Sept. 1st				
1964–65[6]	67.3	700	767	740
1965–66[6]	29.7	844	874	840
RA 1966–67	35.6	931	967	874
1967–68	90.1	973	1063	900
1968–69	166.3	1080	1246	947
1969–70[4]	324.4	1117	1441	1230
1970–71[5]	230.1	1136	1366	1258
1971–72[6]	99.0	1169	1268	1203
1972–73[6]	72.0	1276	1348	1283
RA 1973–74[4]	60.0	1567	1627	1436
1974–75[5]	171.9	1233	1405	1201
1975–76[6]	185.0	1521	1706	1486
1976–77[6]	245.0	1265	1510	1407

RA Relative abundance begins, storage stocks build to a three-year high.

[1]This figure is the December or final figure during the year and often differs from the revised one issued in the following year. The reason for using the December figure rather than the revised figure is that it was the figure that was available at the time trading took place.

[2]Based on the change in mid-September to December usage relative to year before. (After 1953–1954, three and a third times)

Consumption, mid-Sept. to Dec. (5)	Indicated usage[2] (6)	Production compared with indicated usage (7)	Price support (Chicago) (8)	Spring hog production: Increase or decrease (9)
64	—	—	231	+
85	256	+31[3]	226	+
82	295	−14	265	−
87	289	+3	276	−
94	299	−37	276	+
99	298	+48[3]	242	+
120	403	−32	224	−
129	410	+46[3]	235	−
138	473	+7	229	+
155	528	+46[3]	229	+
173	599	−61	205	−
183	605	−46	205	+
187	586	+107[3]	250	−
211[7]	708	−33	245	+
201	679	+23	245	−
232[7]	785	−85	245	−
232[7]	785	−85	245	−
262	840	+4	245	+
264	847	+84[3]	270	+
276	914	+56	270	−
298[7]	973	+107[3]	270	−
362	1160	−43	245	+
378	1283	−147	245	−
352	1171	−2	245	−
405	1380	−104	245	−
411	1303	+264[3]	245	−
358	1259	−26	245	−
435	1458	+63	245	+
448	1531	−269	245	+

[3]8% more.
[4]Anticipatory year; preceding first cut of total supplies after relative abundance (if cut comes during year that begins with relative abundance, anticipatory year precedes first cut in carryover).
[5]Discouragement year; following anticipatory year.
[6]Rationing years; following discouragement year.
[7]Owing to the anticipated dock strike (in January), the December increase in exports from the year before was subtracted.

TABLE 9-2

ANTICIPATORY STAGE AS SEEN IN NOVEMBER CONTRACT

Year	Close April 15	Low close after April 15	High	Close Nov. 8	Net gain (cents)	Dollar profit per contract
1952	271¾	268½	316½	298⅛	+26⅜	1,318
1959	212⅞	208	224¾	223⅜	+10½	525
1963	245⅜	245⅛	291½	288⅞	+43½	2,175
1970	256¾	256⅛	310¼	301¾	+45	2.250
1974	536¼	510¼	956	845½	+309¼	15,462

DISCOURAGEMENT—JULY CONTRACT

Year	Close Nov. 8	High close after Nov. 8	Low	Close May 26	Net break (cents)	
1952–53	303	307⅛	261⅜	285⅛	17⅞	894
1959–60	232¾	231⅞	208⅞	214⅛	18⅝	934
1963–64	302½	300⅛	246¼	248¾	53¾	2,687
1970–71	314⅛	319⅜	289⅝	309¾	46⅜	2,318
1974–75	892½	872½	490	499¼	393¼	19,650

REALIZATION*—JULY CONTRACT

Year	Close June 1	Low close after June 1	High, April to July, fol. yr.	Date	Close June 30	Net gain (cents)	
1953–54	262⅜†	237†	425¾	7/21/54	366⅞	+104½	5,225
1960–61	222†	219⅝†	340	4/26/61	268⅞	+46⅞	2,344
1964–65	252½†	246½†	308¾	4/8/66	296	+43½	2,175
1971–72	313½†	312½	366	4/18/72	348⅜	+35⅞	1,794
1975–76	506	471¾	757	7/7/76	667	+195¼	9,762

SECOND YEAR OF REALIZATION: JULY CONTRACT

Year	Close Dec. 26	Low close after Dec.	High April to July, fol. yr.	Date	Close June 3	Net gain (cents)	
1965–66	272⅞	270⅛	377¼	6/30/66	318⅞	+46	2.300
1972–73	404½	407¼	1290	6/5/73	1211	+806½	40,325
1976–77	694¼	693¾	1064	4/22/77	937	+242¾	12,137

*Second stage of broad bull market.

†On the basis of January contract as July had not yet begun to trade, 8½¢ premium in 1960; 4½¢ premium in 1964; and 6¢ premium in 1971.

Since people had been expecting the usage increase of the preceding year to continue, they became discouraged by the unexpected fall in consumption. As consumption, which had amounted to 711 million bushels in the 1962–1963 crop year, fell to 682 million bushels, a big decline in soybean prices took place. From a high of 304½ during November 1963, the July contract fell to 246½ by the following summer.[6] Let us call this the year of discouragement.

Yet, the lower prices which occurred in this year induced a huge increase in demand in the following crop year while discouraging a sharp increase in production. This disparity led to the second and dynamic stage of the broad bull market. Production for the 1964–1965 crop year was only 2½% more than usage during the 1963–1964 crop year. With consumption in the mid-September-to-December period up 16% from the preceding year, it became apparent that prices would have to rise so that demand could be rationed. As a result, the July soybean contract rallied from a low of 253 in early August of 1964 to 317½ by February of 1965.[7]

In the following crop year, that of 1965–1966, production was sharply expanded, reaching 104 million bushels more than the prior year's consumption. Yet, consumption during the mid-September-to-December period was up 13% from the year before, and, in addition, the effect of the expected increase in the 1966 spring pig crop was yet to be felt. As a result, production was only marginally more—less than 1%—than indicated usage. In the past, it has taken a production increase in excess of 8% to stop the bull market from continuing for two years in succession. Therefore, even though there was a big increase in supplies, we could expect a second year of price rise. From a low of 254¾ in August of 1965, the July soybean contract rallied to 377 by the summer of 1966.[8]

---

[6] Had we sold the July contract on November 8 at 302½ and covered on May 26 at 248½, we would have realized $2687 profit. In addition, we would never have had a loss on that position. (Table 9-2).

[7] Had we bought on June 1 at 252½ and sold on the following June 30 at 296, we would have made $2175 per contract. Also, the biggest loss we would have been subjected to was $300 per contract (Table 9-2).

[8] Had we bought on December 26 at 272⅞ (at which time we could have seen that another big increase in usage was occurring), and sold on June 3 at 318⅞, we would have realized $2300 per contract. During that time, the biggest paper loss we were subjected to was ½¢, or $25 per contract (Table 9-2).

Soybean prices had now experienced a big increase and during the following crop year, that of 1966–1967, a big buildup in supplies materialized, partially induced by the rise in the government price support from $2.45 to $2.70. Production outstripped indicated usage by 10%, a fact that resulted in a big price break and a buildup in the carry-over to 90 million bushels, which was a three-year high. We had now completed one cycle.[9]

Since 1951, there have been four other times when prices broke following a broad bull market and carry-over supplies were built up to a three-year high. Each time that it became apparent, in April of a subsequent crop year, that there would be a cut in total supplies for the following crop year, an anticipatory bull market began and lasted until the following fall. As a result, the next crop year began at a price level that was too high to maintain in the face of a falloff (or milder increase) in consumption. It became a discouragement year wherein prices broke from the fall through the following spring. And following each discouragement year, we got a dynamic advance in prices lasting one to two years.[10] As long as production was no more than marginally higher than indicated usage, say less than 3%, as in 1965, 1972, and 1976, we got a second year in the dynamic advance.

The Storage Egg Market (after 1968, fresh eggs) Owing to an increasing concern about their cholesterol content and the growing popularity of packaged breakfast foods, eggs are experiencing a declining demand. Egg production varies throughout the year because of seasonal shifts in the composition of the laying flock and the rate of lay. From about mid-February until sometime in July, there is usually an excess of supply; in the years before 1968, this surplus was stored either in shell or frozen form. Then, during the September-to-January period, when fresh production falls short of demand, these

---

[9]Had we bought and sold on these designated dates, during this five-year period we would have made $9337 per contract, less commissions.

[10]In the 1975–1976 crop year when production was more than indicated usage, this advance began in May. It became apparent at that time that because of a 10% cut in acreage and bad weather at planting time, production for the following year would be less than the current year's usage.

storage eggs, as they are considered less desirable, are merchandised at a discount from fresh eggs.[11]

Though normally hens can start to lay eggs within six months of being hatched, they do not enter the prime of their productive life until about a year of age. It is at that time that the eggs they lay become large enough to be meaningful. Therefore, chickens hatched in April through August of the previous year have the most significant influence on the fall egg price structure. Those chickens hatched in the following September-to-March period, who thus are six months to a year old during this fall period, play a less important role. By multiplying the previous April–August hatch by two (because of its importance), and adding to this the following September–March hatch (Table 9-3, column 3), we can get a good approximation of our laying flock potential. Changes in this laying flock potential have correlated with changes in the average fall cash egg price—whether it was higher or lower than in the preceding year—in 22 out of 24 years. The only exceptions were in 1958 and 1963, and they differed by only a small amount.

In years that the laying flock potential was larger than the preceding year, we experienced a good-sized bear market in egg futures, and when the flock potential was smaller, we got a bull market (Tables 9-4 and 9-5). Yet, these bull and bear markets were not alike. The 1957, 1958, 1962, and 1963 bull markets fell short of the very large rises occurring in 1955, 1969, 1972, and 1973. And, likewise, the 1961 bear market did not match the other bear markets.

Again we confront a broader cycle. As eggs are a commodity with a declining demand, it experiences recurring broad bear markets. Each of these broad bear markets lasts until we get a major liquidation. A major liquidation occurs when total storage stocks, in equivalent frozen cases[12] on August 1, are greater than they were the year before (see Table 9-3, column 6) in spite of an increase in the size of the laying flock potential. In these years, the increased storage supplies must compete against an increased fresh production and

---

[11]Since 1968 these storage eggs have played a less significant role.

[12]Shell-egg storage stocks are converted to frozen eggs on a basis of 40 pounds per case of eggs and added to frozen egg stocks.

TABLE 9-3   EGG STATISTICS

Year	April–August, previous year (change in millions of hatched chickens) (1)	Following September–March, hatch (change in millions of hatched chickens) (2)	Potential flock: 2 × April–August hatch plus September–March hatch change (in millions of hatched chickens) (3)
1953			
1954*	+29	+63	+121
1955	+11	−77	−55
1956	+1	+21	+23
1957	+2	−79	−75
1958	−64	+13	−115
1959*	+49	+12	+110
1960	−49	−94	−192
1961	+6	+53	+65
1962	−11	−6	−28
1963	0	−3	−3
1964*	+9	+11	+29
1965	−1	−10	−12
1966	−22	+19	−25
1967*	+43	+43	+129
1968 (fresh eggs)	−22	−50	−94
1969	−20	+33	−7
1970	+4	+39	+47
1971*	+22	−16	+28
1972	−5	−34	−44
1973	−31	+10	−52
1974*	+14	+13	+41
1975	−16	−31	−63
1976	−13	−1	−27

*Liquidating years: plus potential flock and plus total storage stocks: four-year September–December cash low.

Total Storage Stocks, August 1			Fall period, August 11– December cash price		Average fall price (9)
Frozen (4)	Frozen equivalent, shell (5)	Total frozen equivalent (6)	Low (7)	High (8)	
(in millions of lb)	(in millions of lb)	(in millions of lb)			
153	48	201	46¢	63¢	54½¢
181	56	237	30*	50	40
195	90	285	43	55	49
177	50	227	31	47	39
177	60	237	38½	52	46¼
140	29	169	33	51	42
152	36	188	27½	45	36¼
166	41	207	33½	55	44¼
113	12	125	30½	43	36¾
122	14	136	35	45½	40¼
108	9	117	34	42	38
114	8	122	28	42	35
98	21	119	33	44½	38¾
62	3	65	37	49½	43¼
93	16	109	26	33	29½
110	10	120	35	53	44
66	8	74	37½	63	50¼
60	6	66	34	47	40½
80	6	86	29	38	33½
88	9	97	29	55	42
48	2	50	58	81	69½
59	4	63	54	70	62
51	4	55	55	73	64
32	1	34	65	80	72½

TABLE 9-4 SMALLER POTENTIAL LAYING FLOCK, DECEMBER CONTRACT

Year	Close 10/29	Lowest close after 10/29	Decline from 10/29	Subsequent high	Date	Close, 2nd-to-last trading day	Price change from 10/29 to 2nd-to-last trading day	Dollar profit on one contract
1955	30.90¢	30.25	.65	46.50	12/19	45.30	+14.40	$2,160
1957	36.65	36.60	.05	41.70	11/25	37.50	+.85	137
1958	32.85	32.40	.45	37.60	12/19	35.50	+2.65	397
1960	38.35	38.05	.30	45.50	11/25	43.35	+5.00	750
1962	29.75	29.60	.15	33.85	12/21	31.85	+2.10	315
1963	33.80	32.00	1.80	36.50	12/23	35.10	+1.30	195
1965	32.85	32.90	—	39.00	12/2	33.80	+.95	142
1966	34.10	34.60	—	40.35	12/2	37.30	+3.20	576

BEGIN FRESH EGGS

Year	Close 3/31	Lowest close after 3/31	Decline from 3/31				Price change from 3/31 to 2nd-to-last trading day	
1968	37.50	37.00	.50	50.25	12/23	49.15	+11.65	$2,097
1969	37.15*	36.50	.65	65.25	12/5	60.40	+23.25	4,185
1972	38.55	36.20	2.35	56.90	12/18	54.65	+16.10	3,622
1973	51.10	49.85	1.25	88.10	8/13	69.60	+18.50	4,162
1975	51.40	50.85	.55	64.95	8/20	60.35	+8.95	2,014
1976	55.10	54.00	1.10	77.30	12/20	75.90	+20.80	4,680

*On the basis of the September contract, as the December contract had not yet begun to trade; the figure reflects the discount available at the end of April for the December contract, which was 0.45¢ in 1969; in 1975 it was a 0.65¢ premium.

therefore eggs suffer a sharp decline in prices—the fall cash low is lower than in the past three fall periods.

Since 1953, there have been six major liquidations: in 1954, 1959, 1964, 1967, 1971, and 1974.[13] These liquidations, by getting rid of marginal producers and putting a prolonged crimp in producers' expansionary tendencies, clear the decks, so to speak. Supplies became temporarily scarce at the same time that demand increased, so that we got a good-sized bull market which lasted one to two years (when the cutback in hatch extended through June of the first bull year, the bull market extended a second year), as shown in Table

---

[13]In 1974, as we were in a period of commodity inflation, eggs did not make a low below that in the last three fall periods. In this case, a break below the low of the preceding fall period was enough to induce a major liquidation.

9-3. This price rise stimulated an increase in the potential laying flock so that a broad bear market began.

The situation became even more bearish than the increase in the potential laying flock would have led us to believe, however. Just as, following a period of sustained economic growth, people become excessively optimistic and perceive an economic future brighter than actually exists, so, following a major price increase in eggs, those in the trade become enthusiastic and do not see that a bullish bias has crept into their statistics. This attitude develops because these major price increases induce a desire by outsiders to enter the business and become producers. In order to satisfy this additional source of demand for baby chicks, new hatcheries spring up. Much of this activity is likely to escape the census taker. The result is an understatement of our supply potential. Also, because we miss the part of current production that is being used to increase our supply potential, we also overstate demand at the same time. So, we do not grasp the extent of the following supply buildup.

TABLE 9-5   LARGER POTENTIAL LAYING FLOCK, JANUARY CONTRACT

Year	Close July 20	Highest close after July 20	Increase from July 20	Subsequent low	Date	Close, following Jan. 8	Price change from July 20 to Jan. 8	Dollar profit on one contract†
1954	41.00¢*	40.25*	—	24.50	12/14	30.00	−11.00	$1,584
1956	39.90	39.40	—	28.45	1/4	29.15	−10.75	1,612
1959	32.70	32.50	—	21.60	1/22	24.70	−8.00	1,200
1961	33.95	35.10	1.15	28.60	12/4	30.85	−3.10	465
1964	33.30*	33.85	.55	21.10	1/22	24.80	−8.50	1,275
1967	38.00*	37.65	—	26.30	1/5	27.75	−10.25	1,845

Begin fresh eggs:

	Close Aug. 16	Highest close after Aug. 16	Increase from Aug. 16			Close, following Jan. 8	Price change from Aug. 16 to Jan. 8	
1970	38.45	39.20	.75	27.45	1/20	34.40	−4.05	$ 850
1971	38.50*	39.90	1.40	27.55	12/30	29.10	−9.40	2,112
1974	64.25	66.30	2.05	51.10	1/6	51.50	−12.75	2,869

*On the basis of the December contract, as January contract had not yet begun to trade, and reflects the January premium available at the end of October; 1.15¢ in 1954; (−20¢) in 1964; 1.20¢ in 1967; and 1.00¢ in 1971.
†Reflects changing size of the contract; 14,400 dozen in 1954; 15,000 dozen in 1955–1965; 18,000 dozen in 1966–1969; 21,000 dozen in 1970; and 22,000 dozen from 1971 to present.

Following each good-sized price rise in the past, a bear market began and lasted until we got another major liquidation. When there was another cutback in flock size during this bear market (as in 1957 and 1962), a secondary bull market followed. However, as these secondary bull markets were not responses to a major liquidation, their price rise was fairly limited. They, in fact, served to restimulate producer optimism so that flocks were rebuilt and the bear market was resumed. Each bear market continued until there was a buildup in storage stocks in the face of a larger flock potential—and the fall cash price fell below the low in the past three autumns.

During an inflationary period (usually during or following a war, especially one which occurs during the second intermediate cycle of the expansionary phase), commodities are usually a good buy, especially those commodities that are experiencing recurring broad bull markets or a growing demand, such as soybeans, sugar, silver, cocoa, and gold. Soybeans went from $3.50 to almost $13 per bushel, or a rise of over $47,000 a contract on a margin of only $1,500, during the 1972–1974 inflationary period. Had we bought soybeans on December 26, 1972, and sold on June 3, 1973 (the traditional time to buy and sell when production, in the year following a dynamic advance, does not exceed indicated usage by 8% or more), we would have made over $40,000 per contract.

During these inflations, almost all commodities experience a big bull market when supplies fall below the inflationary demand.[14] Even eggs would have produced a profit of $4162 per contract during 1973 (Table 9-4).

The best time to buy soybeans has been following a discouragement year (that is, when prices, after having risen in response to a more favorable statistical situation, experienced an unexpected decline that lasted throughout most of the following crop year). Following each of the five discouragement years, supplies could not keep up with the growing demand (new production was less than indicated usage), and we got a dynamic advance (see Tables 7-2 and 7-3). Like soybeans, most other commodities experiencing a growing

---

[14]When the inflationary demand is cut, those commodities with recurring bear markets—or decreasing demand—usually suffer the most pronounced price declines.

demand are a good buy when following a discouragement year there is a noticeable improvement in the supply-and-demand situation.

The mystery in commodities results from the fact that an individual supply and demand situation is affected by a broader cycle, which reflects either diminishing or growing demand. Once we account for this, commodities, because of their frequent cyclical shifts from scarcity to abundance, along with an abundance of good information supplied by reliable government agencies, may be as rewarding as stocks or perhaps (with their smaller margin) even more rewarding.

TEN

THE PSYCHOLOGICAL PITFALL

There is a psychological pitfall which leaves us victims of these cycles. We are misled because our perceptions of the world—that is, whether we see it primarily as a risky or as a not so risky place—are colored by the important lessons of pain and pleasure we experience. As we change our economic behavior to conform to these lessons and rationalize that what has happened will continue to happen, we become committed both economically and psychologically to a risk perception. And, in becoming wedded to a risk perception and the beliefs it has spawned, we tend to bend our judgment and to be slow to accept some contrary evidence. As a result, we are slow to respond to new and changing circumstances—or the changing degrees of real risk in the world. In the late 1920s and again in 1968–1969 it was hard to convince people that this was *not* a time to buy stocks. By the same token, in the late 1940s and again in 1974 when prices were sharply lower, it was hard to talk people into buying stocks. They came up with too many reasons not to.

What happens is this: Following a long period of rising prices in the stock market and again following a sharp collapse in prices, people find it difficult to act contrary to the crowd or not to "go along." They are not able to stand alone and see that at this time the risk (or lack of risk) is more apparent than real.

No matter how prepared we think we are, it is difficult to go against the crowd. Fear of being left behind is a powerful motivator.

Well before the 1929 crash, a number of sophisticated people had recognized the speculative excesses that were occcurring in the stock market and quite properly withdrew. However, as time went on and they saw their former chauffeurs and shoeshine boys pocketing millions, becoming celebrities, and hopping off in expensive limousines with their former mistresses, they were drawn back into the madness. During times of excessive optimism when making money appears easy, the fear of being left at the gate in this mad rush to riches becomes just as great as, or perhaps even greater than, the fear of going down with everyone else in the market.

If we hope to combat this psychological pitfall and avoid becoming one of the crowd, we must be able to adjust to changing degrees of real risk. To do this, the investor needs an economic strategy wherein one views one's economic endeavors as battles in a larger war, never as the war itself. The essence of this economic strategy is to acquire the wherewithal to shift from an offensive to a defensive posture as the situation warrants. This means learning the percentages—the likelihood of certain economic events occurring—so that one may recognize the risks and opportunities. For example, since 1896, each of the five moves into new all-time highs in the stock market occurring after a serious contraction signified that pessimism had abated and once again a significant number of new risk takers were being attracted into the stock market. As a result, each of these new highs were followed by at least a four-year period wherein the risk of owning stocks was quite low.[1]

Those players who adopt an economic strategy confine their actions to the times when the conditions look favorable. When either risk increases or reserves (not only money, but perhaps time and

[1]DOW JONES INDUSTRIAL AVERAGES (RAILROAD AVERAGES IN 1901)

Date	New highs	Four years later	% gain
February 1901	99	123	23
September 1915	82	111	35
December 1924	120	300	150
November 1954	382	557	45
September 1963	737	926	26

TABLE 10-1

	Price: one year before top	Low made during the following serious contraction	% saved
1906	119 DJRA	83	35
1918	85 DJIA	63	25
1928	240 "	41	83
1960	611 "	535	12
1972	912 "	577	35

emotional reserves as well) are lacking, it is necessary to adopt a defensive posture—withdrawing from the field of action and husbanding one's resources while waiting for the confusion to pass. As we have seen, the risk of owning stocks increases as a bull market progresses. The third stage is, of course, the riskiest. Following that stage we get a big break. Had we sold out during it, even as much as a year before the final top was made, we would have saved a great deal of money by being out of the market during the subsequent break (see Table 10-1).

On the other hand, when risk diminishes and opportunity beckons—such as when the stock market makes a new all-time high after a lengthy washout—one should take an offensive posture; that is, one should pursue the field of action in an effort to take advantage of what is happening.

Also, it may be wise to enter a market, not on the basis of being right near term but, rather, when the risk appears to be less. For example, an investor who feels that the market is going much higher in the long term may at times commit some funds to the market even though recognizing that in the near term, the odds favor a lower market. This maneuver—a minor commitment to what one feels is the direction of the longer trend—allows one to sit comfortably through a big rally and not, through fear of missing the boat, to attempt to jump aboard at a level where one has no defense point.

The next consideration is developing a defense point, so that unforeseen events or errors in judgment will not wipe one out. In speculative markets, one miscalculation can offset many years of

canny predictions. In the 1973–1974 stock market break, it was
Morgan Guaranty, which for years had used growth stocks success-
fully, that was caught with too much Avon, Polaroid, Disney, and
other growth stocks. In the two-year period ending September 30,
1974, Morgan's three pooled funds that were geared entirely to such
stocks dropped more than 55% in value, compared with a 38%
decline in the market as measured by Standard & Poor's 500 stock
index. In the same manner, a $5-per-contract loss in the 1973 soy-
bean market, when prices went from $3.50 to nearly $13 ($47,000
per contract), was enough to wipe out 10 years of profits (averaging
50¢ per year) and then some.

To avoid these huge losses one must be able to cut one's losses
short. That is, one must accept a small loss and not wait for the
market to come back and get one out "even." One can accomplish
this goal either by continually reassessing a position whenever it
shows a loss—by asking whether, if one's money were in cold cash,
one would choose the same position—or by placing a stop at some
predetermined point at which the market action indicates that one is
probably wrong. In the latter case, one may need to gain knowledge
of the technical approaches to the market, as they may provide the
best clue to when the market disagrees with the investor's position.

For example, had investors bought shortly after the break of the
1929 low of 198, thinking that a bottom would be made during the
following three-month period (as is usually the case), they should
have expected the low made during this period (157 on the Dow) to
hold.[2] (See Chart 6.) And when the Dow rallied to 194 in early 1931,
it certainly looked as though the stock market had bottomed. However, when the Dow came back and broke this low in April of 1931, it
became apparent that what these investors were expecting to occur
was not happening. At this point, they should have been willing to
admit their error and bail out. Needless to say, the Dow continued to
fall until it hit 41 in June of 1932. Had these investors sold out in
April, they could then have bought back three shares for each one

---

[2]Actually, as we saw earlier, the 1929 low did not qualify as an important low. And,
even if it had qualified, this was the one time in the cycle when such an occurrence
would not provide a real opportunity to buy.

they had sold out. In being willing to give up some, an investor is unlikely to lose all.

The final consideration in this economic strategy is to acquire an adequate amount of reserves. They may be backup capital, outside income, or other people who can be counted on; and these reserves serve as a base of support. As in war or politics, these sources of support provide a player with a strategic advantage. With suitable reserves, setbacks are easier to handle; serious losses are less likely to affect judgment; and when the odds become unfavorable, the player does not have to join in (being in a better position to remain patient until opportunity presents itself).

These reserves enable one to capitalize on changing circumstances. The baseball teams that, some years back, seemed to be doing so well against the powerful Yankees, only to have luck go against them late in the game, were affected by a lack of reserves. Likewise, the lack of such reserves affected Germany's World War II attempt to rescue her crumbling war effort in the Battle of the Bulge. In our surprise at these underdogs' initial success, we seemed to forget that they were spending important reserves, while their more powerful opponent was not. And when something happened—as it usually does[3]—the Yankees or the Allies with their superior reserves were able to take advantage and win once again. It was these superior reserves—not luck or fortuitous circumstances—that were responsible for their triumph.

In a like manner, this is why rich kids who can "count on Daddy" often have an easier time, economically speaking. And members of a stock or commodity exchange, in tacitly developing customs to support one another, have a similar advantage. If one does not develop a base of support, oftentimes nothing else seems to work.

Those people who adhere to an economic strategy live in reality as men and women of action, rather than construct ideal worlds or dream about what ought to be. They are usually better able to adjust to the changing degrees of real risk in our world, and quicker to react to change or to shed theories and opinions that no longer seem to be working. In the Greek play *Antigone*, the chorus warns us, "Not only

---

[3]In a game of cards each player is bound to be dealt some poor hands.

do men move about on a charted landscape. The landscape itself is in constant motion, and men had best be quick enough to move about with it. When they aren't, they go through the cracks that open under their feet."

In a world of shifting environments, the *ability to deal with risk may be more important than acquiring the wherewithal to make superior predictions.* But, because the smart or "superrational" players who stress the importance of developing superior opinions or methods usually do not learn this, they are often unprepared to play in this changing game.

ELEVEN

A SUMMING UP

In presenting various concepts relating to economic and stock market cycles, this book has discussed a number of ideas to strengthen the investor's judgment. A checklist of some of these ideas may help in putting these theories into practice.

A. Determining the end of the expansionary phase of the cycle:

1. Have there been three intermediate cycles in this expansionary phase?

2. Have there been three broad bull markets wherein the stock market made new all-time highs in this expansionary phase?

3. Have long-term interest rates surpassed the natural rate, adjusted for past inflation, and remained above this natural rate through an additional intermediate cycle?

4. Has the secular rise in long-term interest rates and wholesale prices appeared to have peaked or at least leveled off?

5. Has the innovative industry experienced a great deal of growth?

6. Has the expansionary phase been in progress for 30 or more years?

7. Does there appear to be an unbounded optimism along with speculative excesses?

B. Determining the end of the depressionary phase of the cycle:

1. Have there been two intermediate cycles in this depressionary phase?

2. Have there been three broad bear markets in this phase?

3. Have long-term interest rates fallen below the natural rate adjusted for past inflation and remained below the natural rate for about an intermediate cycle?

4. Has the secular fall in long-term interest rates and wholesale prices appeared to have ended?

5. Has there been a dramatic improvement in business earnings?

6. Has this depressionary period been in progress for 18 or more years?

7. Does there appear to be widespread economic pessimism along with a lack of speculative excesses?

C. Anticipating a serious contraction during expansionary times:

1. Have there been three business expansions during this intermediate cycle?[1]

2. Have there been three stages in the corresponding broad bull market in stocks?

3. Have long-term interest rates had a big rise during the business expansion, corresponding to the third stage of the broad bull market?[2]

4. Is there a great deal of speculative activity occurring on the stock exchanges?

---

[1] If the first business expansion of an intermediate cycle is unusually long—say five years or more—and if two stages of the bull market in stocks occurred during that expansion, then there may be only two business expansions. The reason is that the buildup in optimism is occurring during that time.

[2] In the past, long-term interest rates (monthly averages) have risen by at least 13% (usually, over 20%) during this business expansion.

5. Is this period either shortly before the minority party's second try at reelection or shortly after the majority party's second reelection?

D. Anticipating a serious contraction during depressionary times:

1. Has there been a long business expansion accompanied by a rise in stock prices?[3]

2. Are people at least somewhat less cautious than they have been?

E. Recognizing the occurrence of a serious contraction during expansionary times:

1. Has the fall in the Dow Jones Industrial Averages been more severe than in the previous two breaks?

2. Has the Dow broken an important prior low?

3. Has the falloff in industrial production been more severe than in the previous two business contractions?

4. Have long-term interest rates fallen for an extended period (usually 15 months or more)?

5. Have people become more pessimistic as a result of this turndown in business activity?

6. Has it been approximately 12 years from the bottom of the last serious contraction to the bottom of this one?[4]

7. Has there been a change in political parties in the election following this contraction?

F. Recognizing the serious contraction which marks the beginning of the depressionary phase:

1. Has the Dow fallen more than 50% from its highs?

---

[3]In the past, this has been a business expansion of at least three years.

[4]In the past, the time from trough to trough has varied from 11 years to 14 years and 1 month.

2. Has the value of most assets suffered a huge fall?

3. Have business earnings almost vanished?

4. Have long-term interest rates fallen to a very low level?[5]

5. Have wholesale prices suffered a sharp drop?

6. Has this contraction been accompanied by exceedingly high unemployment and lasted close to three years?

G. Recognizing the other serious contractions occurring during the depressionary phase:

1. Has there been a big fall in industrial production?

2. Has there been a big falloff in the Dow?

3. Have long-term interest rates made new lows?

4. Is the following contraction less severe than this contraction?

H. Picking the bottom of the stock market during the expansionary phase:

1. Is this during, or shortly after, a serious contraction?

2. Has the Dow broken an important prior low?

3. Have long-term interest rates made a one-year low during the six months preceding the break of the important prior low?

4. Have people been frightened?

5. Can we expect another stage in the expansionary phase?

6. Does the low of the three months following the break of the prior important low hold?

I. Picking the bottom of the stock market during the depressionary phase:

1. Has the Dow broken an important prior low?

---

[5]The lowest level in over 12 years (the approximate length of an intermediate cycle).

2. Have long-term interest rates made a one-year low during the six months preceding the break of the prior important low?

3. Have people become excessively pessimistic?

4. Does the low of the three months following the break of the prior low hold?

J. Recognizing an important prior low in the stock market:

1. Did this low follow a five-year high?

2. Was it the lowest price in at least 18 months?

3. Did this low hold for a year or more?

K. Picking an important top in the stock market during the expansionary phase:

1. Have there been three stages in this advance (each separated by about a 15% break)?[6]

2. Have there been three business expansions in the corresponding intermediate cycle?[7]

3. Has the Dow gone over the high of the second stage?

4. Has the business expansion corresponding to the third stage progressed for 21 months?

5. Have long-term interest rates had a big rise during the corresponding business expansion?

6. Have people become excessively optimistic?

L. Picking an important top in the stock market during the depressionary phase:

---

[6]While in the past each stage was separated by a break of 15% or more in the Dow, there may be other criteria to determine the end of a stage, such as a 14-month period or more, without the Dow's making a new high.

[7]Maybe only two if the first business expansion is unusually long.

1. Has there been a long advance in stock prices?

2. Have long-term interest rates risen by 10% or more during the first business expansion of the corresponding intermediate cycle?

3. Has the second business expansion of the intermediate cycle been in progress for seven months?

M. Determining when the stock market is vulnerable to a moderately severe break during a broad bull market:

1. Have long-term interest rates exceeded the high made during the prior business expansions?

2. Is this the twenty-sixth month in the life of the first or second stage?

N. Other times to buy during a broad bull market:

1. Has the Dow broken 25% or more?

2. Have long-term interest rates fallen by about 8% or more?

Note: There is usually not too much risk in buying during a broad bull market until about a year or so after the Dow makes new all-time highs. In the past, there was only one time in which the Dow was able to break 25% or more during that period.

O. Other times to sell during a broad bear market:

1. Has the Dow retraced 50% or more of its break?

P. Determining which sector (the blue chips or the growth) is likely to dominate:

1. Are we recovering from a serious contraction and stock market break, wherein the growth stocks suffered a severe fall?

2. Has the Dow made new all-time highs a year or more ago?

3. Has the first stage of the broad bull market been completed?

Q. Picking industries to invest in:

    1. Have the stock prices of an industry broken a previous low during the first or second stage of a broad bull market?

    2. Is this the beginning of a broad bull market?

R. Picking stocks to invest in:

    1. Has the stock made a 12-year low during the first or second stage of the prior broad bull market?

    2. Is this the beginning of a broad bull market?

S. Recognizing a valid growth stock:

    1. What is the innovating industry?[8]

    2. What industries are supporting the innovative industry?

    3. What companies are vying for leadership in these leading industries?

Note: The best time to buy these stocks is usually during the break that follows the first stage of a broad bull market or one year after the Dow makes new all-time highs, whichever comes first.

T. Determining an inflationary period (usually the best time to buy commodities):

    1. Has it been about 36 years since the heart of the last depressionary phase?[9]

    2. Has there been a war, with deficit financing as a consequence?

---

[8]That is, the industry which is providing the cycle with its growth and spawning related industries.

[9]This is usually the time we get our big inflation.

3. Are the Democrats in office, or have they been in office during the past five years?[10]

U. Determining when to buy soybeans:

1. Has there been a cut in total supplies following a buildup in carry-over supplies to a three-year high?

2. Has there been a price rise associated with this cut in supplies followed by a discouragement year?

3. Are supplies in line with (that is, no more than 3% more than) indicated usage?

V. Determining when to buy eggs:

1. Was there a major liquidation (did prices go below the low of the last three fall periods)?

2. Is the laying flock potential less than in the preceding year?

W. Should we attempt to find particular causes for a turn in the cycle?

In looking for a particular economic cause, such as the rise in price of oil being responsible for the serious contraction of 1973–1975, we miss the real reason: that the psychological environment has become overdone. For example, we attempted to explain the tremendous rise in the price of world commodities during 1973–1974 in terms of the Russian wheat purchases, a cutback in the Peruvian anchovy catch (wiping out a critical part of our fishmeal supply, which is used to feed livestock), or a poor fall soybean harvest. Yet, each of these factors had occurred before and was unable to produce price rises anywhere comparable to those that occurred in 1973.

The real explanation for the 1973–1974 explosion in the price of world commodities is that following the long 1948–1969

---

[10]Each of the three inflationary periods of this century began during a Democratic administration and lasted no longer than five years after the Republicans reclaimed the White House.

decline in commodity prices, a psychological environment of pessimism concerning the price prospects of most commodities had become overdone. Too many people had been expecting these low prices to continue and had left the industry, so that our ability to expand supplies was severely cut. Our grain reserves had been pared to the bone. The combined carry-over of wheat, corn, and soybeans, 3454 million bushels in 1961 and 2254 million bushels in 1969, was cut to 1497 million bushels by 1971. And this figure was only part of the picture. Land normally used in agriculture was put to other uses. This change did not show up in the statistics (when acreage controls were lifted, approximately 20 million of the 60 million acres supposedly being held in the soil bank never came back into production).

Owing to this curtailed supply potential, we were no longer able to accommodate the worldwide desire to increase food consumption in 1971 when most of the leading industrial countries were simultaneously undergoing a business expansion. This inability soon produced an explosion in the price of world commodities. (See Chart 13.) Those events, the Russian grain purchases, and the bad fall harvesting weather were able to trigger this adjustment in the price of world commodities—and thus become newsworthy—because they shattered an overdone psychology which was vulnerable to change. Yet, had these particular events not occurred, some other event would have surfaced to serve as the catalyst. Thus, the reasons we see are often not the real reasons. And, on closer examination, acts of God are sometimes acts of Man.

X. What about the tendency of people to catch on?

On Wall Street, once some new relationship is discovered, it no longer works as it had. The players catch on, and in so doing, even out the odds. This evening out of the odds occurs through what is called the discounting process. We can understand how this comes about by looking at what happened once Wall Street became aware of the relationship between money-supply changes and stock prices. Wall Street's attention began focusing on this relationship following the publication of Beryl Sprinkel's book *Money and Stock Prices* in 1964. Dr. Sprinkel contended that bear markets (but for a few misses) were reliably indicated by a contraction in money-supply growth some 12 to 15 months earlier, while bull markets followed an expansion of money supply with a lag of about 2 months. An investor who banked on these relationships, selling stocks 15 months after a contraction in money supply and buying stocks 2 months after an expansion in money supply, would have significantly outperformed a buy-and-hold strategy, according to Dr. Sprinkel.

The first test of this thesis came in 1966. At that time, however, a bear market began at about the same time that money supply began contracting. And the market bottomed eight months later, in October 1966—still six months before the theoretical time to sell. Dr. Sprinkel and his followers, by leisurely awaiting the 15-month lag which had worked so well in the past, would not only have missed the bear market, but would have sold their stocks at the beginning of a new bull market.

What had happened was that once the importance of these money-supply figures became known, each little notch in money-supply contraction (such as a weekly fall) brought forward a group of people who, in thinking we were getting closer to a legitimate money-supply sell signal, were willing to sell then, while prices were still relatively high. This selling helped adjust market prices downward so that by the time the data were, by past standards, conclusive, the market had finished discounting them. As a result, a true money-supply player who waited for confirmation was forced to sell after the occurrence of a sizable break in the stock market. The players had caught on, and their response rendered the 15-month lag that Dr. Sprinkel had discovered practically useless.

Because of this tendency of people to catch on, the establishment and wide distribution of a series of rules lead, so to speak, to their being broken. On the whole, systems or formulas do not work against a fair wheel, for, if they did, they would soon be identified and rendered useless. So, while we have tried to define a way to pick the turning points in these cycles, it is more important to understand this catching-on process: that is, are people becoming excessively optimistic or excessively pessimistic?

Y. Determining whether people are becoming increasingly optimistic or increasingly pessimistic:

1. What is happening to long-term interest rates?

Note: When people are optimistic, they increase their borrowing and spend some of their savings, thus increasing the demand for capital at the same time that the supply of it is lessening, putting upward pressure on long-term interest rates.

On the other hand, when people are pessimistic, they decrease their borrowing and increase their savings, thereby decreasing the demand for capital at the same time that the supply of it is increasing, putting downward pressure on long-term interest rates.

Yet people, by catching on, change economic and stock market trends. Therefore, we must be cognizant of how we are changing the long-term cycle if we are to see what is in store for us.

TWELVE

THE KEYNESIAN REVOLUTION AND OUR FUTURE

The idea of long-term economic cycles suggests that we are in the third stage of a long expansionary phase similar to that during the 1920s. In the not too distant future, this stage should be followed by a period of depression similar to what Great Britain experienced at the end of the last century. However, in the real world, carbon copies are rare. Things are constantly changing, and these long economic cycles are no exception. To get some idea of what the future holds in store for us, we must see how the Keynesian revolution—making the government responsible for maintaining economic growth—has interfered with our simple economic laws and is thus changing the shape of capitalism.

Originally, the Keynesian revolution was an answer to a particular economic malfunction: the long period of insufficient demand which followed an overbuilding of our supplies, i.e., a depression. The problem was that the liquidation of these supplies involved the firing of workers, and thus shattered confidence. Once confidence was destroyed, it took a long time to generate the demand necessary to support any real pickup in economic activity. However, Keynes contended that by giving the government the responsibility to create the purchasing power necessary to regenerate confidence, we could (and, in the interest of humaneness, *should*) put our resources back to work sooner than the natural forces in our economy would dictate, thus ameliorating the depression. This was Keynes's message.

Yet, while the Keynesians may have helped bring us out of an old-

style depression faster and more smoothly than the natural economic forces, and at times they have helped to ameliorate a contraction so that it would be less severe than it might have been,[1] their
policies have helped create another economic malfunction, that is, a
period of excessive demand or insufficient supplies which leads to
an inflation. In stimulating demand via the progressive income tax,
unemployment compensation, social security, welfare payments,
food stamps, and other types of aid to the less advantaged, the
Keynesians have encouraged a huge shift of money and credit from
the investment sphere into the support of consumption. Consequently, it becomes more difficult to finance the investments needed
to expand production: supplies cannot keep up with demand. As a
result, prices rise. Yet, the Keynesians do not let demand respond to
the higher prices by falling, as in theory it should. By increasing
government spending and cutting taxes in order to prevent a politically unfeasible credit collapse along with a serious rise in unemployment, the Keynesians end up accommodating these inflationary
price and wage increases. Thus, Keynesian economics has left us
with a structural vulnerability to inflation.

The Keynesian revolution, with its accompanying inflationary
bias, is changing the way our economic cycles work. The enormous
falloffs in the price level and interest rates that accompanied our
past depressionary periods *are likely to occur no more.* At best, we
may expect a moderate decline in the price level for a rather short
period of time. In the last cycle, in contrast with prior cycles,
wholesale prices bottomed in 1939, well before the end of the
depressionary period, and they have had a steeper and more pronounced rise since then (see Chart 1). And, the serious contraction of

---

[1]Until the mid-1960s, Keynesian formulas worked reasonably well. The first two
serious contractions since the government took an active role in influencing economic
activity, those of 1945–1946, and 1960–1961, were the least severe of all our serious
contractions. Except for the damage they created in the financial markets, their effect
was not much more than a milder recession. However, in the mid-1960s, when the
psychological environment changed to one in which most people became optimistic,
the Keynesian formulas no longer worked. At that time, government efforts to stimulate the economy were likely to fuel an inflation, which in turn was soon followed by a
business contraction, and these business contractions became more serious than they
had been.

1973–1975 led to a leveling off of the price level, rather than an actual decline like that occurring in 1920–1921. Also, as we have already begun to see, the problem of cooling expectations and defusing social tensions becomes more difficult in this age of inflation.

The result is that the third intermediate cycle of this expansionary phase is likely to entail more inflation and less stability, both political and social, then in the 1920s. In fact, our chief problem this time around may be this inability to get inflation under control. In that case, the excessive speculation which normally occurs at the end of a cycle may be more prevalent in real estate, commodities, and other hedges against inflation than in the stock market. Also, the rise in long-term interest rates may be more pronounced at that time than in the late 1920s—perhaps even exceeding the high reached in 1974.

In the next depressionary phase, the demands brought on by our long cyclical expansion must be cooled and many of our excessive economic commitments liquidated, if we are to experience another long period of expansion. Yet, in an age of inflation, how are we going to cool demands and keep both interest rates and the price level stable?

According to the "gold bugs," a group of economic cynics who were among the first and most vocal to catch on to the inability of Keynesian economics to deal with inflation, the solution is quite simple: Return to the discipline of gold. This approach means returning control over our economy to an impersonal metal and thus putting an end to the Keynesian attempt to tamper with our economy. Of course, we would be putting the economy "through the wringer"—that is, accepting a deflation with its accompanying unemployment—any time the increase in the actual supply of gold lags behind the buildup in the dollar value of goods.

What the gold bugs do not reckon with, however, is that the Keynesian revolution was no accident. It was able to transform nineteenth-century capitalism into our modern "managed economy" because it implemented the growing belief that a society governed by people of reason *does not have to tolerate* economic pain.

This belief is a product of our historical experience. Just as a long period of prosperity leads to rising economic expectations, so an important historical experience may also change the way we view the world. Nearly 400 years ago, when Galileo came forth to back up the Copernican theory that the sun was the center of our universe with rigorous proofs based on empirical verification, the Age of Reason was born. As the scientific developments which followed showed that people could indeed dominate nature and the industrial revolution arrived, people began to see themselves as more powerful than before. They came to believe that they had acquired the wherewithal to control their own destiny, that they were to be blessed with continued industrial progress. With this conviction began a revolution of rising expectations.

This discovery of reason led to a broad upheaval in our outlook. The perception of an unfriendly world which characterized the Dark and Middle Ages gave way to one in which people became optimistic that they could derive pleasure in "this world."[2] In such an environment, people who have the vote are not about to go back and tie us to a "cross of gold"—at least not for long.[3]

So, when faced with a time of troubles, the same factor that led to the Keynesian revolution—the belief that we had acquired the rational and monetary resources to mitigate economic pain—is likely to transform capitalism to a more completely managed or controlled economy. Such a society is not likely to reward those (the "gold bugs") who have bet against it.

In the next depressionary period, it is likely that the government will be forced to increase the scope of its involvement in our economy in order to alleviate unemployment, keep our troubled industries (and local governments) afloat, and protect pensions and mortgages which are likely to be placed in jeopardy. This government action means extending the benefits of a welfare state, nationalizing some industries and, in general, extending our thrust toward socialism. As a result, the economy may show a marked improvement after

---

[2]This same worldly outlook seems also to have occurred in Greek and Roman times when an increase in commerce brought a higher level of abundance to those in the upper tiers of society.

[3]Because a society, in such an environment, cannot remain indifferent to the moral and psychological torture which accompanies mass unemployment merely because of the beneficial long-term economic effects, our notion of a "free" economy is a fiction. Economics is, and for most of our history has been, subservient to politics.

passing the heart of the depressionary phase wherein some of our excesses are liquidated; that is, the fifth intermediate cycle of the current super cycle may be measurably more prosperous than the 1940s.[4]

Yet, as this depressionary period should be more mild and less of a humbling experience than the previous one, the problem we will have to face is the one of controlling behavior. It seems that, in the past, our recurring economic lesson of pain—depressions—served to control behavior and keep demands reasonable. The pain that depressions induced discouraged the personal greed and corruption and the transgressions of authority which surfaced during times of heightened economic expectations, and led men to subordinate their self-interest to the welfare of the "community."[5] As a result of dampening the role that economic pain plays in curbing the demands which build during the expansionary phase, we are likely to encroach further on the extent of liberty that our political system allows. As we saw in Russia, China, Chile, and Cuba, an economy cannot be controlled without putting limits on personal freedom. To cool demands in the international arena—by the third world, or by some other nation—we may have to accept another type of pain or more bloodshed. We saw this happen during our last depressionary period which, toward the end, was dominated by World War II rather than by depression.[6] In the next depressionary period, it may again be necessary to send American youth or bombers to some corner of the world in order to counter aggression.

Our real time of troubles, though, rather than coming during the next depressionary period, is likely to be reserved for the following

---

[4]As the psychological environment changes again to one in which most people are pessimistic, Keynesian formulas will probably be able to work once again. The first two serious contractions of that psychological environment may be fairly mild, as in 1945–1946 and 1960–1961. This moderation may be another legacy of the Keynesian revolution.

[5]In fact, it appears that because our economic cycles periodically provided a lesson of pain, we were able to do away with political controls and develop a political system in which we became liberated—democracy.

[6]A war coming after the heart of the depressionary phase may be a consequence of our reluctance to accept a high level of economic pain: potential aggressors are not humbled.

expansionary phase—or the third American cycle. By then we will probably have vastly increased the amount of government debt as a result of providing economic protection such as pensions, welfare, and social security during the depressionary phase, thus further adding to our capital shortage. It is also likely that, owing to our unwillingness to develop and apply a new form of power, our technology will lag, and this, in turn, will further constrain our ability to expand production. Also, by then, in order to prevent the Fed from undercutting the government's fight against the earlier depression, we are likely to have canceled its political independence. Thus we would remove our last remaining bulwark against a really serious inflation.

So, with a shortage of capacity, and no one left to say no to the increasing demands which accompany heightened expectations, there is a good chance that during the expansionary phase of the next economic cycle, we will experience our great inflation, somewhat similar to what occurred in France in the late eighteenth century or Germany in the 1920s. Both those hyperinflations developed during a leading country's third cycle, as she was being challenged by a contender. (While in the first instance the hyperinflation occurred in the leading country, France, in the later case it took place in the challenging country, Germany.)

These hyperinflations serve to abort our cyclical expansions. They do so because savers no longer save, workers desert the labor market and seek fast money-making schemes. As we saw earlier, this trend further hinders the capital formation process. In addition, the galloping prices, along with the excessive social tensions that accompany these inflations, increase the demand for economic and political controls. Such controls, when enacted, impede the very same innovational process that was responsible for our economic prosperity.

Not only do hyperinflations cut short cyclical expansions, but also they pose a threat to the workings of a capitalistic society. The reason is that, with its wealth eaten away by inflation, the middle class, the traditional stabilizing element of a democratic society, loses its stake in the social order. As order breaks down owing to the difficulty of controlling people during times of escalating prices, people lose their trust in traditional authority. They become more likely to buy leaders who will impose political controls to achieve economic stability and social order.

Let us look at the classic case of an inflation that got out of hand, that of post-World War I Germany. Because of the heavy borrowing needed in order to finance her war effort and the war reparations that had to be paid under the Versailles Treaty, Germany had become a huge debtor nation. In addition, the Left attained political control and its leaders were reluctant to impose the harsh economic measures needed to cool the inflationary demands—political, social, and economic—which surfaced after the First World War. The German contraction of 1920–1921 was rather mild, compared with what happened in most other major economic nations. People did not experience a lesson of economic pain.[7] As demands escalated, the level of social strife and abrasiveness mounted, order broke down or seemed to as street battles or assassinations became almost daily occurrences, and as prices rose at an increasingly faster pace, the purchasing power of wages vanished. By October 1923, one needed trillions of marks to buy a loaf of bread or mail a letter, the rate of interest reached 10,000 percent (the person lending 1 mark one year would get back 10,001 marks the following year). Manufacturing fell sharply, farmers refused to ship their produce, workers hovered near starvation, food riots broke out, and millions of the middle class, watching their money become worthless, were forced to sell household goods, family artifacts, or real estate, in order to eat.

While inflation was brought under control in 1924 as a new currency was introduced, the budget brought into balance, and the Dawes plan[8] proposed, the anger and frustration of the deposed middle class remained. This class, many members of which had trusted in their government and had skimped and saved, were left without a penny and had lost their stake in the social order. Authority had been unable to protect them. They had seen order break down and their values trampled on. Berlin became a Babylon of the 1920s wherein bars, amusement parks, and pubs shot up like mush-

---

[7]A smaller lesson.

[8]Under this plan, the French were to leave the Ruhr, Germany's reparations payments were considerably reduced, and, to meet these payments, Germany was to receive loans.

rooms, every sort of perversion and debauchery flourished, and people's savings vanished while speculators grew rich.

So, in the early 1930s, when the economy became depressed and it looked as though Germany were headed for a repeat of the earlier economic and social instability, the middle class was ready to back a leader who promised economic stability and a firm hand to tame the noisemakers and keep order—at the mere price of their political liberty.

The Keynesians, of course, are not too concerned with such a threat. They back up their arguments by pointing to the examples of Brazil and Japan who, while experiencing high rates of inflation, were able to produce considerable economic growth and to emerge with their political and social foundations intact. However, their experience may not be relevant for us: Secondary countries have the means of coping with these hyperinflations that is denied leading countries. First, secondary countries are able to imitate or copy the leading country, so that economic innovation does not play such an important role. Next, the middle class, or many members of it, by finding a safe haven for its money outside the country, is able to protect its wealth, as well as its place in society. Also, a *rigid social structure* often helps the middle class keep its stake in the social order. Finally, these secondary countries may already have *political controls*, a force which helps keep the social and economic demands which accompany inflations reasonable.

Without these outlets of a secondary nation, a hyperinflation is likely to lead to excessive political controls in order to restore order or bring behavior under control. The crisis usually occurs in some internal upheaval or revolution. As such, a hyperinflation may, on balance, prove to be more bloodletting than a depression. Lord Keynes himself said, "There is no subtler, no surer means of overturning the basis of society than to debauch the currency. The process engages all the hidden forces of economic law on the side of destruction."

The bias in capitalism is in the process of shifting from *insufficient demand* to *insufficient supplies*. As a result, in the future our chief problem is likely to be *serious inflation*, rather than depressions.

GLOSSARY OF TERMS FREQUENTLY USED

anticipatory stage   A price move based upon some expected event that has not yet occurred.

blue chip stocks   Stocks of the leading companies in those industries that had established an important role in the American economy prior to the current expansionary period.

broad bear market   A long, usually two-staged, decline in stock prices such as occurred from 1937–1942.

broad bull market   A long, three-staged advance in stock prices, with each stage separated by an approximate 15% break in prices. An example is the long rise in stock prices from 1962–1973.

business expansion   The traditional two- to four-year upswing in economic activity.

crop year   The period of producing and marketing one crop.

depression   A business contraction which is unusually severe.

depressionary phase   A long period of time during which business contractions are especially severe.

discount   To take an expected future event into account and incorporate it into the price structure.

discount rate   The interest rate the Federal Reserve Bank charges to its member banks.

discouragement stage A price decline following a rise based on an expected favorable occurrence.

dominant industry The leading industry, which usually provides the innovational impetus to an expansionary phase.

excessive optimism When people think there is less risk in the economy than actually exists and do not display the proper caution.

excessive pessimism When people think there is more risk in the economy than actually exists and are extremely cautious.

expansionary phase A long period wherein business activity during each smaller business expansion surpasses the level achieved during the preceding business expansion, and wherein business contractions are not too severe.

Fed A commonly used shortened form for the Federal Reserve Board.

growth stocks The stocks of those companies of a new industry that are experiencing superior rates of growth.

heart of the depressionary phase Usually the period that encompasses the first two serious contractions of the depressionary phase.

hyperinflation A very serious inflation, resembling the one that occurred in Germany during the 1920s.

intermediate cycle A series of traditional business expansions followed by a serious contraction.

liquidity Savings and liquid assets which can be converted into cash almost immediately.

long-term economic cycle An approximate 54-year cycle of economic activity which goes from bust to boom to bust again.

margin The amount of money that must be deposited with a broker as a guarantee of payment for the purchase of a security.

natural rate of interest   The supposed rate of return on capital (after inflation has been subtracted).

price-earnings ratio   The current price of a share of stock divided by the annual earnings per share.

prior important low   An important low which, by our definition, follows a five-year high. It is the lowest price in at least 18 months and holds for a year or more before being broken.

psychological environment   The psychology of the majority of people, whether they see the world as risky and are trying to avoid pain, or as not risky and are attempting to pursue pleasure.

psychology of affluence   When people see the world as not so risky and their dominant theme becomes the pursuit of pleasure. In the economic sphere, they are optimistic.

psychology of deflation   When people see the world as risky and their dominant theme becomes the avoidance of pain. In the economic sphere, they are pessimistic.

recession   A business contraction which is usually defined as two consecutive quarters of no real growth in the GNP (gross national product).

risk averter   Someone who is not willing to depend upon an expanding economy for his or her well-being. This definition includes salaried employees and bureaucrats as well as those who delay consumption so that they may build up the level of their savings.

risk taker   Someone who attempts to take advantage of a growing economy. This term includes entrepreneurs and speculators as well as those who adopt a standard of living which does not leave much room for savings.

serious contraction   A contraction which is more severe than the others. These contractions are usually accompanied by a huge falloff in industrial activity, a sharp break in the stock market, and an extended decline in long-term interest rates.

speculative stocks   Stocks of those companies that are currently in the process of proving, or failing to prove, themselves.

stimulative inflation   An inflation resulting from a sharp expansion in money supply which usually occurs at the end of the depressionary phase and helps stimulate business to move out of the mire of depression.

stop order   An order which is executed only if the market reaches the level mentioned in the order.

INDEX